HBR'S 10 MUST READS

On
Organizational
Resilience

HBR's 10 Must Reads series is the definitive collection of ideas and best practices for aspiring and experienced leaders alike. These books offer essential reading selected from the pages of *Harvard Business Review* on topics critical to the success of every manager.

Titles include:

HBR's 10 Must Reads 2015
HBR's 10 Must Reads 2016
HBR's 10 Must Reads 2017
HBR's 10 Must Reads 2018
HBR's 10 Must Reads 2019
HBR's 10 Must Reads 2020
HBR's 10 Must Reads 2021
HBR's 10 Must Reads for CEOs
HBR's 10 Must Reads for New Managers
HBR's 10 Must Reads on AI, Analytics, and the New Machine Age
HBR's 10 Must Reads on Boards
HBR's 10 Must Reads on Building a Great Culture
HBR's 10 Must Reads on Business Model Innovation
HBR's 10 Must Reads on Change Management
HBR's 10 Must Reads on Collaboration
HBR's 10 Must Reads on Communication
HBR's 10 Must Reads on MR Creativity
HBR's 10 Must Reads on Design Thinking
HBR's 10 Must Reads on Diversity
HBR's 10 Must Reads on Emotional Intelligence
HBR's 10 Must Reads on Entrepreneurship and Startups
HBR's 10 Must Reads on Innovation
HBR's 10 Must Reads on Leadership
HBR's 10 Must Reads on Leadership (Vol. 2)
HBR's 10 Must Reads on Leadership for Healthcare
HBR's 10 Must Reads on Leadership Lessons from Sports
HBR's 10 Must Reads on Making Smart Decisions

On
Organizational
Resilience

HARVARD BUSINESS REVIEW PRESS
Boston, Massachusetts

Copyright 2021 Harvard Business School Publishing Corporation

The web addresses referenced in this book were live and correct at the time of the book's publication but may be subject to change.

Cataloging-in-Publication data is forthcoming.

ISBN: 978-1-64782-068-8
eISBN: 978-1-64782-069-5

Contents

HBR'S 10 MUST READS

On
Organizational
Resilience

How Resilience Works

by Diane L. Coutu

WHEN I BEGAN MY CAREER in journalism—I was a reporter at a national magazine in those days—there was a man I'll call Claus Schmidt. He was in his mid-fifties, and to my impressionable eyes, he was the quintessential newsman: cynical at times, but unrelentingly curious and full of life, and often hilariously funny in a sandpaper-dry kind of way. He churned out hard-hitting cover stories and features with a speed and elegance I could only dream of. It always astounded me that he was never promoted to managing editor.

But people who knew Claus better than I did thought of him not just as a great newsman but as a quintessential survivor, someone who had endured in an environment often hostile to talent. He had lived through at least three major changes in the magazine's leadership, losing most of his best friends and colleagues on the way. At home, two of his children succumbed to incurable illnesses, and a third was killed in a traffic accident. Despite all this—or maybe because of it—he milled around the newsroom day after day, mentoring the cub reporters, talking about the novels he was writing—always looking forward to what the future held for him.

Why do some people suffer real hardships and not falter? Claus Schmidt could have reacted very differently. We've all seen that happen: One person cannot seem to get the confidence back after a layoff; another, persistently depressed, takes a few years off from life after her divorce. The question we would all like answered is, Why? What exactly is that quality of resilience that carries people through life?

It's a question that has fascinated me ever since I first learned of the Holocaust survivors in elementary school. In college, and later in my studies as an affiliate scholar at the Boston Psychoanalytic Society and Institute, I returned to the subject. For the past several months, however, I have looked on it with a new urgency, for it seems to me that the terrorism, war, and recession of recent months have made understanding resilience more important than ever. I have considered both the nature of individual resilience and what makes some organizations as a whole more resilient than others. Why do some people and some companies buckle under pressure? And what makes others bend and ultimately bounce back?

My exploration has taught me much about resilience, although it's a subject none of us will ever understand fully. Indeed, resilience is one of the great puzzles of human nature, like creativity or the religious instinct. But in sifting through psychological research and in reflecting on the many stories of resilience I've heard, I have seen a little more deeply into the hearts and minds of people like Claus Schmidt and, in doing so, looked more deeply into the human psyche as well.

The Buzz About Resilience

Resilience is a hot topic in business these days. Not long ago, I was talking to a senior partner at a respected consulting firm about how to land the very best MBAs—the name of the game in that particular industry. The partner, Daniel Savageau (not his real name), ticked off a long list of qualities his firm sought in its hires: intelligence, ambition, integrity, analytic ability, and so on. "What about resilience?" I asked. "Well, that's very popular right now," he said. "It's the new buzzword. Candidates even tell us they're resilient; they volunteer the information. But frankly, they're just too young to know that about themselves. Resilience is something you realize you have *after* the fact."

Idea in Brief

These are dark days: people are losing jobs, taking pay cuts, suffering foreclosure on their homes. Some of them are snapping—sinking into depression or suffering a permanent loss of confidence.

But others are snapping back; for example, taking advantage of a layoff to build a new career. What carries them through tough times? Resilience.

Resilient people possess three defining characteristics: They coolly accept the harsh realities facing them. They find meaning in terrible times. And they have an uncanny ability to improvise, making do with whatever's at hand.

In deep recessions, resilience becomes more important than ever. Fortunately, you can learn to be resilient.

"But if you could, would you test for it?" I asked. "Does it matter in business?"

Savageau paused. He's a man in his late forties and a success personally and professionally. Yet it hadn't been a smooth ride to the top. He'd started his life as a poor French Canadian in Woonsocket, Rhode Island, and had lost his father at six. He lucked into a football scholarship but was kicked out of Boston University twice for drinking. He turned his life around in his twenties, married, divorced, remarried, and raised five children. Along the way, he made and lost two fortunes before helping to found the consulting firm he now runs. "Yes, it does matter," he said at last. "In fact, it probably matters more than any of the usual things we look for." In the course of reporting this article, I heard the same assertion time and again. As Dean Becker, the president and CEO of Adaptiv Learning Systems, a four-year-old company in King of Prussia, Pennsylvania, that develops and delivers programs about resilience training, puts it: "More than education, more than experience, more than training, a person's level of resilience will determine who succeeds and who fails. That's true in the cancer ward, it's true in the Olympics, and it's true in the boardroom."

Academic research into resilience started about 40 years ago with pioneering studies by Norman Garmezy, now a professor emeritus at the University of Minnesota in Minneapolis. After studying why

Idea in Practice

Resilience can help you survive and recover from even the most brutal experiences. To cultivate resilience, apply these practices.

Face Down Reality

Instead of slipping into denial to cope with hardship, take a sober, down-to-earth view of the reality of your situation. You'll prepare yourself to act in ways that enable you to endure—training yourself to survive before the fact.

> *Example:* Admiral Jim Stockdale survived being held prisoner and tortured by the Vietcong in part by accepting he could be held for a long time. (He was held for eight years.) Those who didn't make it out of the camps kept optimistically assuming

they'd be released on shorter timetables—by Christmas, by Easter, by the Fourth of July. "I think they all died of broken hearts," Stockdale said.

Search for Meaning

When hard times strike, resist any impulse to view yourself as a victim and to cry, "Why me?" Rather, devise constructs about your suffering to create meaning for yourself and others. You'll build bridges from your present-day ordeal to a fuller, better future. Those bridges will make the present manageable, by removing the sense that the present is overwhelming.

> *Example:* Austrian psychiatrist and Auschwitz survivor Victor Frankl realized that to survive

many children of schizophrenic parents did not suffer psychological illness as a result of growing up with them, he concluded that a certain quality of resilience played a greater role in mental health than anyone had previously suspected.

Today, theories abound about what makes resilience. Looking at Holocaust victims, Maurice Vanderpol, a former president of the Boston Psychoanalytic Society and Institute, found that many of the healthy survivors of concentration camps had what he calls a "plastic shield." The shield was comprised of several factors, including a sense of humor. Often the humor was black, but nonetheless it provided a critical sense of perspective. Other core characteristics that helped included the ability to form attachments to others and the possession of an inner psychological space that protected the survivors from the intrusions of abusive others. Research about other

the camp, he had to find some purpose. He did so by imagining himself giving a lecture after the war on the psychology of the concentration camp to help outsiders understand what he had been through. By creating concrete goals for himself, he rose above the sufferings of the moment.

Continually Improvise

When disaster hits, be inventive. Make the most of what you have, putting resources to unfamiliar uses and imagining possibilities others don't see.

Example: Mike founded a business with his friend Paul, selling educational materials to schools, businesses, and consulting firms. When a recession hit, they lost many core clients. Paul went through a bitter divorce, suffered a depression, and couldn't work. When Mike offered to buy him out, Paul slapped him with a lawsuit claiming Mike was trying to steal the business.

Mike kept the company going any way he could—going into joint ventures to sell English-language training materials to Russian and Chinese competitors, publishing newsletters for clients, and even writing video scripts for competitors. The lawsuit was eventually settled in his favor, and he had a new and much more solid business than the one he started out with.

groups uncovered different qualities associated with resilience. The Search Institute, a Minneapolis-based nonprofit organization that focuses on resilience and youth, found that the more resilient kids have an uncanny ability to get adults to help them out. Still other research showed that resilient inner-city youth often have talents such as athletic abilities that attract others to them.

Many of the early theories about resilience stressed the role of genetics. Some people are just born resilient, so the arguments went. There's some truth to that, of course, but an increasing body of empirical evidence shows that resilience—whether in children, survivors of concentration camps, or businesses back from the brink—can be learned. For example, George Vaillant, the director of the Study of Adult Development at Harvard Medical School in Boston, observes that within various groups studied during a 60-year period, some people became markedly more resilient over their lifetimes. Other psychologists claim that unresilient people more easily develop resiliency skills than those with head starts.

Most of the resilience theories I encountered in my research make good common sense. But I also observed that almost all the theories overlap in three ways. Resilient people, they posit, possess three characteristics: a staunch acceptance of reality; a deep belief, often buttressed by strongly held values, that life is meaningful; and an uncanny ability to improvise. You can bounce back from hardship with just one or two of these qualities, but you will only be truly resilient with all three. These three characteristics hold true for resilient organizations as well. Let's take a look at each of them in turn.

Facing Down Reality

A common belief about resilience is that it stems from an optimistic nature. That's true but only as long as such optimism doesn't distort your sense of reality. In extremely adverse situations, rose-colored thinking can actually spell disaster. This point was made poignantly to me by management researcher and writer Jim Collins, who happened upon this concept while researching *Good to Great*, his book on how companies transform themselves out of mediocrity. Collins had a hunch (an exactly wrong hunch) that resilient companies were filled with optimistic people. He tried out that idea on Admiral Jim Stockdale, who was held prisoner and tortured by the Vietcong for eight years.

Collins recalls: "I asked Stockdale: 'Who didn't make it out of the camps?' And he said, 'Oh, that's easy. It was the optimists. They were the ones who said we were going to be out by Christmas. And then they said we'd be out by Easter and then out by Fourth of July and out by Thanksgiving, and then it was Christmas again.' Then Stockdale turned to me and said, 'You know, I think they all died of broken hearts.'"

In the business world, Collins found the same unblinking attitude shared by executives at all the most successful companies he studied.

Like Stockdale, resilient people have very sober and down-to-earth views of those parts of reality that matter for survival. That's not to say that optimism doesn't have its place: In turning around a demoralized sales force, for instance, conjuring a sense of possibility can be a very powerful tool. But for bigger challenges, a cool, almost pessimistic, sense of reality is far more important.

Perhaps you're asking yourself, "Do I truly understand—and accept—the reality of my situation? Does my organization?" Those are good questions, particularly because research suggests most people slip into denial as a coping mechanism. Facing reality, really facing it, is grueling work. Indeed, it can be unpleasant and often emotionally wrenching. Consider the following story of organizational resilience, and see what it means to confront reality.

Prior to September 11, 2001, Morgan Stanley, the famous investment bank, was the largest tenant in the World Trade Center. The company had some 2,700 employees working in the south tower on 22 floors between the 43rd and the 74th. On that horrible day, the first plane hit the north tower at 8:46 a.m., and Morgan Stanley started evacuating just one minute later, at 8:47 a.m. When the second plane crashed into the south tower 15 minutes after that, Morgan Stanley's offices were largely empty. All told, the company lost only seven employees despite receiving an almost direct hit.

Of course, the organization was just plain lucky to be in the second tower. Cantor Fitzgerald, whose offices were hit in the first attack, couldn't have done anything to save its employees. Still, it was Morgan Stanley's hard-nosed realism that enabled the company to benefit from its luck. Soon after the 1993 attack on the World Trade Center, senior management recognized that working in such a symbolic center of U.S. commercial power made the company vulnerable to attention from terrorists and possible attack.

With this grim realization, Morgan Stanley launched a program of preparedness at the micro level. Few companies take their fire drills seriously. Not so Morgan Stanley, whose VP of security for the Individual Investor Group, Rick Rescorla, brought a military discipline to the job. Rescorla, himself a highly resilient, decorated Vietnam vet, made sure that people were fully drilled about what to do in a catastrophe. When disaster struck on September 11, Rescorla was on a bullhorn telling Morgan Stanley employees to stay calm and follow their well-practiced drill, even though some building supervisors were telling occupants that all was well. Sadly, Rescorla himself, whose life story has been widely covered in recent months, was one of the seven who didn't make it out.

"When you're in financial services where so much depends on technology, contingency planning is a major part of your business," says President and COO Robert G. Scott. But Morgan Stanley was prepared for the very toughest reality. It had not just one, but three, recovery sites where employees could congregate and business could take place if work locales were ever disrupted. "Multiple backup sites seemed like an incredible extravagance on September 10," concedes Scott. "But on September 12, they seemed like genius."

Maybe it was genius; it was undoubtedly resilience at work. The fact is, when we truly stare down reality, we prepare ourselves to act in ways that allow us to endure and survive extraordinary hardship. We train ourselves how to survive before the fact.

The Search for Meaning

The ability to see reality is closely linked to the second building block of resilience, the propensity to make meaning of terrible times. We all know people who, under duress, throw up their hands and cry, "How can this be happening to me?" Such people see themselves as victims, and living through hardship carries no lessons for them. But resilient people devise constructs about their suffering to create some sort of meaning for themselves and others.

I have a friend I'll call Jackie Oiseaux who suffered repeated psychoses over a 10-year period due to an undiagnosed bipolar disorder. Today, she holds down a big job in one of the top publishing companies in the country, has a family, and is a prominent member of her church community. When people ask her how she bounced back from her crises, she runs her hands through her hair. "People sometimes say, 'Why me?' But I've always said, 'Why *not* me?' True, I lost many things during my illness," she says, "but I found many more—incredible friends who saw me through the bleakest times and who will give meaning to my life forever."

This dynamic of meaning making is, most researchers agree, the way resilient people build bridges from present-day hardships to a fuller, better constructed future. Those bridges make the present manageable, for lack of a better word, removing the sense that the present is overwhelming. This concept was beautifully articulated by Viktor E. Frankl, an Austrian psychiatrist and an Auschwitz survivor. In the midst of staggering suffering, Frankl invented "meaning therapy," a humanistic therapy technique that helps individuals make the kinds of decisions that will create significance in their lives.

In his book *Man's Search for Meaning*, Frankl described the pivotal moment in the camp when he developed meaning therapy. He was on his way to work one day, worrying whether he should trade his last cigarette for a bowl of soup. He wondered how he was going to work with a new foreman whom he knew to be particularly sadistic. Suddenly, he was disgusted by just how trivial and meaningless his life had become. He realized that to survive, he had to find some purpose. Frankl did so by imagining himself giving a lecture after the war on the psychology of the concentration camp, to help outsiders understand what he had been through. Although he wasn't even sure he would survive, Frankl created some concrete goals for himself. In doing so, he succeeded in rising above the sufferings of the moment. As he put it in his book: "We must never forget that we may also find meaning in life even when confronted with a hopeless situation, when facing a fate that cannot be changed."

Frankl's theory underlies most resilience coaching in business. Indeed, I was struck by how often businesspeople referred to his work. "Resilience training—what we call hardiness—is a way for us to help people construct meaning in their everyday lives," explains Salvatore R. Maddi, a University of California, Irvine psychology professor and the director of the Hardiness Institute in Newport Beach, California. "When people realize the power of resilience training, they often say, 'Doc, is this what psychotherapy is?' But psychotherapy is for people whose lives have fallen apart badly and need repair. We see our work as showing people life skills and attitudes. Maybe those things should be taught at home, maybe they should be taught in schools, but they're not. So we end up doing it in business."

Yet the challenge confronting resilience trainers is often more difficult than we might imagine. Meaning can be elusive, and just because you found it once doesn't mean you'll keep it or find it again. Consider Aleksandr Solzhenitsyn, who survived the war against the Nazis, imprisonment in the gulag, and cancer. Yet when he moved to a farm in peaceful, safe Vermont, he could not cope with the "infantile West." He was unable to discern any real meaning in what he felt to be the destructive and irresponsible freedom of the West. Upset by his critics, he withdrew into his farmhouse, behind a locked fence, seldom to be seen in public. In 1994, a bitter man, Solzhenitsyn moved back to Russia.

Since finding meaning in one's environment is such an important aspect of resilience, it should come as no surprise that the most successful organizations and people possess strong value systems. Strong values infuse an environment with meaning because they offer ways to interpret and shape events. While it's popular these days to ridicule values, it's surely no coincidence that the most resilient organization in the world has been the Catholic Church, which has survived wars, corruption, and schism for more than 2,000 years, thanks largely to its immutable set of values. Businesses that survive also have their creeds, which give them purposes beyond just making money. Strikingly, many companies describe their value systems in religious terms. Pharmaceutical giant Johnson & Johnson, for instance, calls its value system, set out in a document given to every new employee at orientation, the Credo. Parcel company UPS talks constantly about its Noble Purpose.

Value systems at resilient companies change very little over the years and are used as scaffolding in times of trouble. UPS Chairman and CEO Mike Eskew believes that the Noble Purpose helped the company to rally after the agonizing strike in 1997. Says Eskew: "It was a hugely difficult time, like a family feud. Everyone had close friends on both sides of the fence, and it was tough for us to pick sides. But what saved us was our Noble Purpose. Whatever side people were on, they all shared a common set of values. Those values are core to us and never change; they frame most of our important decisions. Our strategy and our mission may change, but our values never do."

The religious connotations of words like "credo," "values," and "noble purpose," however, should not be confused with the actual content of the values. Companies can hold ethically questionable values and still be very resilient. Consider Phillip Morris, which has demonstrated impressive resilience in the face of increasing unpopularity. As Jim Collins points out, Phillip Morris has very strong values, although we might not agree with them—for instance, the value of "adult choice." But there's no doubt that Phillip Morris executives believe strongly in its values, and the strength of their beliefs sets the company apart from most of the other tobacco companies. In this context, it is worth noting that resilience is neither ethically good nor bad. It is merely the skill and the capacity to be robust under conditions of enormous stress and change. As Viktor Frankl wrote: "On the average, only those prisoners could keep alive who, after years of trekking from camp to camp, had lost all scruples in their fight for existence; they were prepared to use every means, honest and otherwise, even brutal . . . in order to save themselves. We who have come back . . . we know: The best of us did not return."

Values, positive or negative, are actually more important for organizational resilience than having resilient people on the payroll. If resilient employees are all interpreting reality in different ways, their decisions and actions may well conflict, calling into doubt the survival of their organization. And as the weakness of an organization becomes apparent, highly resilient individuals are more likely to jettison the organization than to imperil their own survival.

Ritualized Ingenuity

The third building block of resilience is the ability to make do with whatever is at hand. Psychologists follow the lead of French anthropologist Claude Levi-Strauss in calling this skill bricolage.[1] Intriguingly, the roots of that word are closely tied to the concept of resilience, which literally means "bouncing back." Says Levi-Strauss: "In its old sense, the verb *bricoler* . . . was always used with reference to some extraneous movement: a ball rebounding, a dog straying, or a horse swerving from its direct course to avoid an obstacle."

Bricolage in the modern sense can be defined as a kind of inventiveness, an ability to improvise a solution to a problem without proper or obvious tools or materials. *Bricoleurs* are always tinkering—building radios from household effects or fixing their own cars. They make the most of what they have, putting objects to unfamiliar uses. In the concentration camps, for example, resilient inmates knew to pocket pieces of string or wire whenever they found them. The string or wire might later become useful—to fix a pair of shoes, perhaps, which in freezing conditions might make the difference between life and death.

When situations unravel, bricoleurs muddle through, imagining possibilities where others are confounded. I have two friends, whom I'll call Paul Shields and Mike Andrews, who were roommates throughout their college years. To no one's surprise, when they graduated, they set up a business together, selling educational materials to schools, businesses, and consulting firms. At first, the company was a great success, making both founders paper millionaires. But the recession of the early 1990s hit the company hard, and many core clients fell away. At the same time, Paul experienced a bitter divorce and a depression that made it impossible for him to work. Mike offered to buy Paul out but was instead slapped with a lawsuit claiming that Mike was trying to steal the business. At this point, a less resilient person might have just walked away from the mess. Not Mike. As the case wound through the courts, he kept the company going any way he could—constantly morphing the business until he found a model that worked: going into joint ventures to sell English-language training materials to Russian and Chinese companies. Later, he branched off into publishing newsletters for clients. At one point, he was even writing video scripts for his competitors. Thanks to all this bricolage, by the time the lawsuit was settled in his favor, Mike had an entirely different, and much more solid, business than the one he had started with.

Bricolage can be practiced on a higher level as well. Richard Feynman, winner of the 1965 Nobel Prize in physics, exemplified what I like to think of as intellectual bricolage. Out of pure curiosity,

Feynman made himself an expert on cracking safes, not only looking at the mechanics of safecracking but also cobbling together psychological insights about people who used safes and set the locks.
He cracked many of the safes at Los Alamos, for instance, because
he guessed that theoretical physicists would not set the locks with
random code numbers they might forget but would instead use
a sequence with mathematical significance. It turned out that the
three safes containing all the secrets to the atomic bomb were set to
the same mathematical constant, e, whose first six digits are 2.71828.

Resilient organizations are stuffed with bricoleurs, though not all
of them, of course, are Richard Feynmans. Indeed, companies that
survive regard improvisation as a core skill. Consider UPS, which
empowers its drivers to do whatever it takes to deliver packages on
time. Says CEO Eskew: "We tell our employees to get the job done.
If that means they need to improvise, they improvise. Otherwise we
just couldn't do what we do every day. Just think what can go wrong:
a busted traffic light, a flat tire, a bridge washed out. If a snowstorm
hits Louisville tonight, a group of people will sit together and discuss how to handle the problem. Nobody tells them to do that. They
come together because it's our tradition to do so."

That tradition meant that the company was delivering parcels in
southeast Florida just one day after Hurricane Andrew devastated
the region in 1992, causing billions of dollars in damage. Many people
were living in their cars because their homes had been destroyed,
yet UPS drivers and managers sorted packages at a diversion site and
made deliveries even to those who were stranded in their cars. It was
largely UPS's improvisational skills that enabled it to keep functioning after the catastrophic hit. And the fact that the company continued on gave others a sense of purpose or meaning amid the chaos.

Improvisation of the sort practiced by UPS, however, is a far cry
from unbridled creativity. Indeed, much like the military, UPS lives
on rules and regulations. As Eskew says: "Drivers always put their
keys in the same place. They close the doors the same way. They
wear their uniforms the same way. We are a company of precision." He believes that although they may seem stifling, UPS's rules
were what allowed the company to bounce back immediately after

Hurricane Andrew, for they enabled people to focus on the one or two fixes they needed to make in order to keep going.

Eskew's opinion is echoed by Karl E. Weick, a professor of organizational behavior at the University of Michigan Business School in Ann Arbor and one of the most respected thinkers on organizational psychology. "There is good evidence that when people are put under pressure, they regress to their most habituated ways of responding," Weick has written. "What we do not expect under life-threatening pressure is creativity." In other words, the rules and regulations that make some companies appear less creative may actually make them more resilient in times of real turbulence.

Claus Schmidt, the newsman I mentioned earlier, died about five years ago, but I'm not sure I could have interviewed him about his own resilience even if he were alive. It would have felt strange, I think, to ask him, "Claus, did you really face down reality? Did you make meaning out of your hardships? Did you improvise your recovery after each professional and personal disaster?" He may not have been able to answer. In my experience, resilient people don't often describe themselves that way. They shrug off their survival stories and very often assign them to luck.

Obviously, luck does have a lot to do with surviving. It was luck that Morgan Stanley was situated in the south tower and could put its preparedness training to work. But being lucky is not the same as being resilient. Resilience is a reflex, a way of facing and understanding the world, that is deeply etched into a person's mind and soul. Resilient people and companies face reality with staunchness, make meaning of hardship instead of crying out in despair, and improvise solutions from thin air. Others do not. This is the nature of resilience, and we will never completely understand it.

Originally published in May 2002. **Reprint** R0205B

Note

1. See, e.g., Karl E. Weick, "The Collapse of Sense-making in Organizations: The Mann Gulch Disaster," *Administrative Science Quarterly*, December 1993.

The Quest for Resilience

by Gary Hamel and Liisa Välikangas

CALL IT THE resilience gap. The world is becoming turbulent faster than organizations are becoming resilient. The evidence is all around us. Big companies are failing more frequently. Of the 20 largest U.S. bankruptcies in the past two decades, 10 occurred in the last two years. Corporate earnings are more erratic. Over the past four decades, year-to-year volatility in the earnings growth rate of S&P 500 companies has increased by nearly 50%—despite vigorous efforts to "manage" earnings. Performance slumps are proliferating. In each of the years from 1973 to 1977, an average of 37 *Fortune* 500 companies were entering or in the midst of a 50%, five-year decline in net income; from 1993 to 1997, smack in the middle of the longest economic boom in modern times, the average number of companies suffering through such an earnings contraction more than doubled, to 84 each year.

Even perennially successful companies are finding it more difficult to deliver consistently superior returns. In their 1994 best-seller *Built to Last*, Jim Collins and Jerry Porras singled out 18 "visionary" companies that had consistently outperformed their peers between 1950 and 1990. But over the last 10 years, just six of these companies managed to outperform the Dow Jones Industrial Average. The other 12—a group that includes companies like Disney, Motorola, Ford, Nordstrom, Sony, and Hewlett-Packard—have apparently gone from great to merely OK. Any way you cut it, success has never been so fragile.

In less turbulent times, established companies could rely on the flywheel of momentum to sustain their success. Some, like AT&T and American Airlines, were insulated from competition by regulatory protection and oligopolistic practices. Others, like General Motors and Coca-Cola, enjoyed a relatively stable product paradigm—for more than a century, cars have had four wheels and a combustion engine and consumers have sipped caffeine-laced soft drinks. Still others, like McDonald's and Intel, built formidable first-mover advantages. And in capital-intensive industries like petroleum and aerospace, high entry barriers protected incumbents.

The fact that success has become less persistent strongly suggests that momentum is not the force it once was. To be sure, there is still enormous value in having a coterie of loyal customers, a well-known brand, deep industry know-how, preferential access to distribution channels, proprietary physical assets, and a robust patent portfolio. But that value has steadily dissipated as the enemies of momentum have multiplied. Technological discontinuities, regulatory upheavals, geopolitical shocks, industry deverticalization and disintermediation, abrupt shifts in consumer tastes, and hordes of nontraditional competitors—these are just a few of the forces undermining the advantages of incumbency.

In the past, executives had the luxury of assuming that business models were more or less immortal. Companies always had to work to get better, of course, but they seldom had to get different—not at their core, not in their essence. Today, getting different is the imperative. It's the challenge facing Coca-Cola as it struggles to raise its "share of throat" in noncar-bonated beverages. It's the task that bedevils McDonald's as it tries to rekindle growth in a world of burger-weary customers. It's the hurdle for Sun Microsystems as it searches for ways to protect its high-margin server business from the Linux onslaught. And it's an imperative for the big pharmaceutical companies as they confront declining R&D yields, escalating price pressure, and the growing threat from generic drugs. For all these companies, and for yours, continued success no longer hinges on momentum. Rather, it rides on resilience—on the ability to dynamically reinvent business models and strategies as circumstances change.

Idea in Brief

Corporate success has never been so fragile. Technology break-throughs, regulatory upheavals, geopolitical shocks—these are just a few of the forces undermining today's business models. With the world growing increasingly turbulent, perennially successful companies are failing. Corporate earnings are whipsawing. Performance slumps are proliferating.

Firms can no longer count on the flywheel of momentum and incumbency to sustain performance. Instead, they need **strategic resilience:** the ability to dynamically reinvent business models and strategies as circum-stances change, to continuously anticipate and adjust to changes that threaten their core earning power—and to change *before* the need becomes desperately obvi-ous.

The quest for resilience starts with these bold aspirations: a strategy that's forever morphing in re-sponse to emerging opportunities and trends; an organization that's constantly remaking its future rather than defending its past; a company where revolutionary change comes in lightning-quick, evolutionary steps—with no ca-lamitous surprises, indiscriminate layoffs, or colossal write-offs.

Fantastical, you say? Not if your company addresses four major challenges.

Strategic resilience is not about responding to a onetime crisis. It's not about rebounding from a setback. It's about continuously anticipating and adjusting to deep, secular trends that can perma-nently impair the earning power of a core business. It's about having the capacity to change before the case for change becomes desper-ately obvious.

Zero Trauma

Successful companies, particularly those that have enjoyed a rela-tively benign environment, find it extraordinarily difficult to rein-vent their business models. When confronted by paradigm-busting turbulence, they often experience a deep and prolonged reversal of fortune. Consider IBM. Between 1990 and 1993, the company went from making $6 billion to losing nearly $8 billion. It wasn't until

Idea in Practice

Any organization striving for strategic resilience must master four challenges:

Conquer denial. Though warning signs of dramatically changing circumstances abound, many of us refuse to acknowledge them because the implications are unpalatable. To boost your corporate resilience, replace "That can't be true" with "We must face the world as it is." Become deeply conscious of what's changing—and perpetually consider how those changes might affect your firm's current success. Here's how:

- Witness change close-up—and often. Visit cutting-edge labs, talk with fervent activists—and anyone under 18. Ask, "What are the potential consequences of the changes I'm seeing?"

- Find out who in your organization is plugged into the future and understands its implications for your business model. Ensure that they have access to you. Go out to dinner with your most freethinking employees. Talk with potential customers who aren't buying from you. Review proposals that *don't* make it to the top.

- Acknowledge that your company's strategy will inevitably get replicated by rivals, supplanted by better strategies, exhausted as markets become saturated, or eviscerated when power shifts to new players.

Value variety. Variety is insurance against the unexpected. Instead of making a single billion-dollar bet, launch a swarm of $10,000-$20,000 bets—smaller, lower-risk

---

1997 that its earnings reached their previous high. Such a protracted earnings slump typically provokes a leadership change, and in many cases the new CEO—be it Gerstner at IBM or Ghosn at Nissan or Bravo at Burberry—produces a successful, if wrenching, turnaround. However celebrated, a turnaround is a testament to a company's lack of resilience. A turnaround is transformation tragically delayed.

Imagine a ratio where the numerator measures the magnitude and frequency of strategic transformation and the denominator reflects the time, expense, and emotional energy required to effect that transformation. Any company that hopes to stay relevant in a topsy-turvy world has no choice but to grow the numerator. The real trick is to steadily reduce the denominator at the same time. To thrive in turbulent times, companies must become as efficient at renewal as

experiments. Thousands of ideas will produce dozens of promising ones that may yield a few huge successes. Test promising ideas through prototypes, computer simulations, and customer interviews. Most experiments will fail. But it's your experiment *portfolio's* performance that matters.

Example:

When domestic-appliance maker Whirlpool invited 10,000 of its 65,000 employees to brainstorm product breakthroughs, they generated 7,000+ ideas that spawned 300 small-scale experiments. Results? A stream of new products—from Gladiator Garage Works (modular storage units) to the Gator Pak (an all-in-one food and entertainment center for tailgate parties).

Liberate resources. To avoid over-funding moribund strategies, get cash to people who can bring new ideas to fruition. Create an investment market inside your firm by giving everyone who controls a budget the ability to provide seed funding for ideas aimed at transforming the core business. "Investors" could form syndicates to take on bigger risks or diversify their "portfolios."

Embrace paradox. Dedicate as much energy to systematic exploration of new strategic options as you do to the relentless pursuit of efficiency. Reward people for strategic variety, wide-scale experimentation, and rapid resource deployment. Your reward? An organization that responds to change continuously—without destructive turmoil.

they are at producing today's products and services. Renewal must be the natural consequence of an organization's innate resilience.

The quest for resilience can't start with an inventory of best practices. Today's best practices are manifestly inadequate. Instead, it must begin with an aspiration: zero trauma. The goal is a strategy that is forever morphing, forever conforming itself to emerging opportunities and incipient trends. The goal is an organization that is constantly making its future rather than defending its past. The goal is a company where revolutionary change happens in lightning-quick, evolutionary steps—with no calamitous surprises, no convulsive reorganizations, no colossal write-offs, and no indiscriminate, across-the-board layoffs. In a truly resilient organization, there is plenty of excitement, but there is no trauma.

Sound impossible? A few decades ago, many would have laughed at the notion of "zero defects." If you were driving a Ford Pinto or a Chevy Vega, or making those sorry automobiles, the very term would have sounded absurd. But today we live in a world where Six Sigma, 3.4 defects per million, is widely viewed as an achievable goal. So why shouldn't we commit ourselves to zero trauma? Defects cost money, but so do outdated strategies, missed opportunities, and belated restructuring programs. Today, many of society's most important institutions, including its largest commercial organizations, are not resilient. But no law says they must remain so. It is precisely because resilience is such a valuable goal that we must commit ourselves to making it an attainable one. (See the sidebar "Why Resilience Matters.")

Any organization that hopes to become resilient must address four challenges:

The Cognitive Challenge: A company must become entirely free of denial, nostalgia, and arrogance. It must be deeply conscious of what's changing and perpetually willing to consider how those changes are likely to affect its current success.

The Strategic Challenge: Resilience requires alternatives as well as awareness—the ability to create a plethora of new options as compelling alternatives to dying strategies.

The Political Challenge: An organization must be able to divert resources from yesterday's products and programs to tomorrow's. This doesn't mean funding flights of fancy; it means building an ability to support a broad portfolio of breakout experiments with the necessary capital and talent.

The Ideological Challenge: Few organizations question the doctrine of optimization. But optimizing a business model that is slowly becoming irrelevant can't secure a company's future. If renewal is to become continuous and opportunity-driven, rather than episodic and crisis-driven, companies will need to embrace a creed that extends beyond operational excellence and flawless execution.

Few organizations, if any, can claim to have mastered these four challenges. While there is no simple recipe for building a resilient organization, a decade of research on innovation and renewal allows us to suggest a few starting points.

Conquering Denial

Every business is successful until it's not. What's amazing is how often top management is surprised when "not" happens. This astonishment, this belated recognition of dramatically changed circumstances, virtually guarantees that the work of renewal will be significantly, perhaps dangerously, postponed.

Why the surprise? Is it that the world is not only changing but changing in ways that simply cannot be anticipated—that it is *shockingly* turbulent? Perhaps, but even "unexpected" shocks can often be anticipated if one is paying close attention. Consider the recent tech sector meltdown—an event that sent many networking and computer suppliers into a tailspin and led to billions of dollars in write-downs.

Three body blows knocked the stuffing out of IT spending: The telecom sector, traditionally a big buyer of networking gear, imploded under the pressure of a massive debt load; a horde of dot-com customers ran out of cash and stopped buying computer equipment; and large corporate customers slashed IT budgets as the economy went into recession. Is it fair to expect IT vendors to have anticipated this perfect storm? Yes.

They knew, for example, that the vast majority of their dot-com customers were burning through cash at a ferocious rate but had no visible earnings. The same was true for many of the fledgling telecom outfits that were buying equipment using vendor financing. These companies were building fiber-optic networks far faster than they could be utilized. With bandwidth increasing more rapidly than demand, it was only a matter of time before plummeting prices would drive many of these debt-heavy companies to the wall. There were other warning signs. In 1990, U.S. companies spent 19% of their capital budgets on information technology. By 2000, they were devoting 59% of their capital spending to IT. In other words, IT had tripled its share of capital budgets—this during the longest capital-spending boom in U.S. history. Anyone looking at the data in 2000 should have been asking, Will capital spending keep growing at a double-digit pace? And is it likely that IT spending will continue

Why Resilience Matters

SOME MIGHT ARGUE that there is no reason to be concerned with the resilience of any particular company as long as there is unfettered competition, a well-functioning market for corporate ownership, a public policy regime that doesn't protect failing companies from their own stupidity, and a population of startups eager to exploit the sloth of incumbents. In this view, competition acts as a spur to perpetual revitalization. A company that fails to adjust to its changing environment soon loses its relevance, its customers, and, ultimately, the support of its stakeholders. Whether it slowly goes out of business or gets acquired, the company's human and financial capital gets reallocated in a way that raises the marginal return on those assets.

This view of the resilience problem has the virtue of being conceptually simple. It is also simpleminded. While competition, new entrants, takeovers, and bankruptcies are effective as purgatives for managerial incompetence, these forces cannot be relied on to address the resilience problem efficiently and completely. There are several reasons why.

First, and most obvious, thousands of important institutions lie outside the market for corporate control, from privately owned companies like Cargill to public-sector agencies like Britain's National Health Service to nonprofits like the Red Cross. Some of these institutions have competitors; many don't. None of them can be easily "taken over." A lack of resilience may go uncorrected for a considerable period of time, while constituents remain underserved and society's resources are squandered.

Second, competition, acquisitions, and bankruptcies are relatively crude mechanisms for reallocating resources from poorly managed companies to well-managed ones. Let's start with the most draconian of these alternatives—bankruptcy. When a firm fails, much of its accumulated intellectual capital disintegrates as teams disperse. It often takes months or years for labor markets to redeploy displaced human assets. Takeovers are a more efficient reallocation mechanism, yet they, too, are a poor substitute for organizational resilience. Executives in underperforming companies, eager to protect their privileges and prerogatives, will typically resist the idea of a takeover until all other survival options have been exhausted. Even then, they are likely to significantly underestimate the extent of institutional decay—a misjudgment that is often shared by the acquiring company. Whether it be Compaq's acquisition of a stumbling Digital Equipment Corporation or Ford's takeover of the deeply troubled Jaguar, acquisitions often prove to be belated, and therefore expensive, responses to institutional decline.

And what about competition, the endless warfare between large and small, old and young? Some believe that as long as a society is capable of creating new organizations, it can afford to be unconcerned about the resilience of old institutions. In this ecological view of resilience, the population of start-ups constitutes a portfolio of experiments, most of which will fail but a few of which will turn into successful businesses.

In this view, institutions are essentially disposable. The young eat the old. Leaving aside for the moment the question of whether institutional longevity has a value in and of itself, there is a reason to question this "who needs dumb, old incumbents when you have all these cool start-ups" line of reasoning. Young companies are generally less efficient than older companies—they are at an earlier point on the road from disorderly innovation to disciplined optimization. An economy composed entirely of start-ups would be grossly inefficient. Moreover, start-ups typically depend on established companies for funding, managerial talent, and market access. Classically, Microsoft's early success was critically dependent on its ability to harness IBM's brand and distribution power. Start-ups are thus not so much an alternative to established incumbents, as an insurance policy against the costs imposed on society by those incumbents that prove themselves to be unimaginative and slow to change. As is true in so many other situations, avoiding disaster is better than making a claim against an insurance policy once disaster has struck. Silicon Valley and other entrepreneurial hot spots are a boon, but they are no more than a partial solution to the problem of non-adaptive incumbents.

To the question, Can a company die an untimely death? an economist would answer no. Barring government intervention or some act of God, an organization fails when it deserves to fail, that is, when it has proven itself to be consistently unsuccessful in meeting the expectations of its stakeholders. There are, of course, cases in which one can reasonably say that an organization "deserves" to die. Two come immediately to mind: when an organization has fulfilled its original purpose or when changing circumstances have rendered the organization's core purpose invalid or no longer useful. (For example, with the collapse of Soviet-sponsored communism in Eastern Europe, some have questioned the continued usefulness of NATO.)

But there are cases in which organizational death should be regarded as premature in that it robs society of a future benefit. Longevity is important because time enables complexity. It took millions of years for biological evolution to produce the complex structures of the mammalian eye and millions more for it to develop the human brain and higher consciousness. Likewise, it takes years, sometimes decades, for an organization to elaborate a simple idea into a robust operational model. Imagine for a moment that Dell, cur-

Why Resilience Matters (*continued*)

rently the world's most successful computer maker, had died in infancy. It is at least possible that the world would not now possess the exemplary "build-to-order" business model Dell so successfully constructed over the past decade—a model that has spurred supply chain innovation in a host of other industries. This is not an argument for insulating a company from its environment; it is, however, a reason to imbue organizations with the capacity to dynamically adjust their strategies as they work to fulfill their long-term missions.

There is a final, noneconomic, reason to care about institutional longevity, and therefore resilience. Institutions are vessels into which we as human beings pour our energies, our passions, and our wisdom. Given this, it is not surprising that we often hope to be survived by the organizations we serve. For if our genes constitute the legacy of our individual, biological selves, our institutions constitute the legacy of our collective, purposeful selves. Like our children, they are our progeny. It is no wonder that we hope they will do well and be well treated by our successors. This hope for the future implies a reciprocal responsibility—that we be good stewards of the institutions we have inherited from our forebears. The best way of honoring an institutional legacy is to extend it, and the best way to extend it is to improve the organization's capacity for continual renewal.

Once more, though, we must be careful. A noble past doesn't entitle an institution to an illustrious future. Institutions deserve to endure only if they are capable of withstanding the onslaught of new institutions. A society's freedom to create new institutions is thus a critical insurance policy against its inability to recreate old ones. Where this freedom has been abridged as in, say, Japan, managers in incumbent institutions are able to dodge their responsibility for organizational renewal.

---

to grow so fast? Logically, the answer to both questions had to be no. Things that can't go on forever usually don't. IT vendors should have anticipated a major pullback in their revenue growth and started "war gaming" postboom options well before demand collapsed.

It is unfair, of course, to single out one industry. What happened to a few flat-footed IT companies can happen to any company—and often does. More than likely, Motorola was startled by Nokia's quick sprint to global leadership in the mobile phone business; executives at the Gap probably received a jolt when, in early 2001, their company's growth engine suddenly went into reverse; and CNN's

Revolution, Renewal, and Resilience: A Glossary for Turbulent Times

WHAT'S THE PROBABILITY THAT YOUR COMPANY will significantly outperform the world economy over the next few years? What's the chance that your company will deliver substantially better returns than the industry average? What are the odds that change, in all its guises, will bring your company considerably more upside than downside? Confidence in the future of your business—or of any business—depends on the extent to which it has mastered three essential forms of innovation.

Revolution

In most industries it's the revolutionaries—like JetBlue, Amgen, Costco, University of Phoenix, eBay, and Dell—that have created most of the new wealth over the last decade. Whether newcomer or old timer, a company needs an unconventional strategy to produce unconventional financial returns. Industry revolution is creative destruction. It is innovation with respect to industry rules.

Renewal

Newcomers have one important advantage over incumbents—a clean slate. To reinvent its industry, an incumbent must first reinvent itself. Strategic renewal is creative reconstruction. It requires innovation with respect to one's traditional business model.

Resilience

It usually takes a performance crisis to prompt the work of renewal. Rather than go from success to success, most companies go from success to failure and then, after a long, hard climb, back to success. Resilience refers to a capacity for continuous reconstruction. It requires innovation with respect to those organizational values, processes, and behaviors that systematically favor perpetuation over innovation.

---

management team was undoubtedly surprised by the Fox News Channel's rapid climb up the ratings ladder.

But they, like those in the IT sector, should have been able to see the future's broad outline—to anticipate the point at which a growth curve suddenly flattens out or a business model runs out of steam. The fact that serious performance shortfalls so often come as a surprise suggests that executives frequently take refuge in denial. Greg Blonder, former chief technical adviser at AT&T, admitted as much in a November 2002 *Barron's* article: "In the early 1990s, AT&T management argued internally that the steady upward curve of Internet usage would somehow collapse. The idea that it might actually overshadow traditional telephone service was simply unthinkable. But the trend could not be stopped—or even slowed—by wishful thinking and clever marketing. One by one, the props that held up the long-distance business collapsed." For AT&T, as for many other companies, the future was less unknowable than it was unthinkable, less inscrutable than unpalatable.

Denial puts the work of renewal on hold, and with each passing month, the cost goes up. To be resilient, an organization must dramatically reduce the time it takes to go from "that can't be true" to "we must face the world as it is." So what does it take to break through the hard carapace of denial? Three things.

First, senior managers must make a habit of visiting the places where change happens first. Ask yourself how often in the last year you have put yourself in a position where you had the chance to see change close-up—where you're weren't reading about change in a business magazine, hearing about it from a consultant, or getting a warmed-over report from an employee, but were experiencing it firsthand. Have you visited a nanotechnology lab? Have you spent a few nights hanging out in London's trendiest clubs? Have you spent an afternoon talking to fervent environmentalists or antiglobalization activists? Have you had an honest, what-do-you-care-about conversation with anyone under 18? It's easy to discount secondhand data; it's hard to ignore what you've experienced for yourself. And if you have managed to rub up against what's changing, how much time have you spent thinking through the second- and third-order consequences of what you've witnessed? As the rate of change increases, so must the personal energy you devote to understanding change.

Second, you have to filter out the filterers. Most likely, there are people in your organization who are plugged tightly in to the future and understand well the not-so-sanguine implications for your company's business model. You have to find these people. You have to make sure their views are not censored by the custodians of convention and their access is not blocked by those who believe they are paid to protect you from unpleasant truths. You should be wary of anyone who has a vested interest in your continued ignorance, who fears that a full understanding of what's changing would expose his own failure to anticipate it or the inadequacy of his response.

There are many ways to circumvent the courtiers and the self-protecting bureaucrats. Talk to potential customers who aren't buying from you. Go out for drinks and dinner with your most freethinking employees. Establish a shadow executive committee whose members are, on average, 20 years younger than the "real" executive committee. Give this group of 30-somethings the chance to review capital budgets, ad campaigns, acquisition plans, and divisional strategies—and to present their views directly to the board. Another strategy is to periodically review the proposals that never made it to the top—those that got spiked by divisional VPs and unit managers. Often it's what doesn't get sponsored that turns out to be most in tune with what's changing, even though the proposals may be out of tune with prevailing orthodoxies.

Finally, you have to face up to the inevitability of strategy decay. On occasion, Bill Gates has been heard to remark that Microsoft is always two or three years away from failure. Hyperbole, perhaps, but the message to his organization is clear: Change will render irrelevant at least some of what Microsoft is doing today—and it will do so sooner rather than later. While it's easy to admit that nothing lasts forever, it is rather more difficult to admit that a dearly beloved strategy is rapidly going from ripe to rotten.

Strategies decay for four reasons. Over time they get *replicated*; they lose their distinctiveness and, therefore, their power to produce above-average returns. Ford's introduction of the Explorer may have established the SUV category, but today nearly every carmaker—from Cadillac to Nissan to Porsche—has a high-standing, gas-guzzling monster in its product line. No wonder Ford's profitability has recently taken a hit. With a veritable army of consultants hawking best practices and a bevy of business journalists working to uncover the secrets of high-performing companies, great ideas get

Anticipating Strategy Decay

BUSINESS STRATEGIES DECAY IN FOUR WAYS—by being replicated, supplanted, exhausted, or eviscerated. And across the board, the pace of strategy decay is accelerating. The following questions, and the metrics they imply, make up a panel of warning lights that can alert executives to incipient decline.

The fact that renewal so often lags decay suggests that corporate leaders regularly miss, or deny, the signs of strategy decay. A diligent, honest, and frequent review of these questions can help to remedy this situation.

Replication

Is our strategy losing its distinctiveness?

Does our strategy defy industry norms in any important ways?

Do we possess any competitive advantages that are truly unique?

Is our financial performance becoming less exceptional and more average?

Supplantation

Is our strategy in danger of being superseded?

Are there discontinuities (social, technical, or political) that could significantly reduce the economic power of our current business model?

---

replicated faster than ever. And when strategies converge, margins collapse.

Good strategies also get *supplanted* by better strategies. Whether it's made-to-order PCs à la Dell, flat-pack furniture from IKEA, or downloadable music via KaZaA, innovation often undermines the earning power of traditional business models. One company's creativity is another's destruction. And in an increasingly connected economy, where ideas and capital travel at light speed, there's every reason to believe that new strategies will become old strategies ever more quickly.

Strategies get *exhausted* as markets become saturated, customers get bored, or optimization programs reach the point of diminishing returns. One example: In 1995, there were approximately 91 million active mobile phones in the world. Today, there are more than 1 billion. Nokia rode this growth curve more adeptly than any of its

Are there nascent business models that might render ours irrelevant?

Do we have strategies in place to co-opt or neutralize these forces of change?

Exhaustion
Is our strategy reaching the point of exhaustion?

Is the pace of improvement in key performance metrics (cost per unit or marketing expense per new customer, for example) slowing down?

Are our markets getting saturated; are our customers becoming more fickle?

Is our company's growth rate decelerating, or about to start doing so?

Evisceration
Is increasing customer power eviscerating our margins?

To what extent do our margins depend on customer ignorance or inertia?

How quickly, and in what ways, are customers gaining additional bargaining power?

Do our productivity improvements fall to the bottom line, or are we forced to give them back to customers in the form of lower prices or better products and services at the same price?

---

rivals. At one point its market value was three-and-a-half times that of its closest competitor. But the number of mobile phones in the world is not going to increase by 1,000% again, and Nokia's growth curve has already started to flatten out. Today, new markets can take off like a rocket. But the faster they grow, the sooner they reach the point where growth begins to decelerate. Ultimately, every strategy exhausts its fuel supply.

Finally, strategies get *eviscerated*. The Internet may not have changed everything, but it has dramatically accelerated the migration of power from producers to consumers. Customers are using their newfound power like a knife, carving big chunks out of once-fat margins. Nowhere has this been more evident than in the travel business, where travelers are using the Net to wrangle the lowest possible prices out of airlines and hotel companies. You know all those e-business efficiencies your company has been reaping? It's going to end up giving most of those productivity gains back to customers in the form of lower prices or better products and services at the same price. Increasingly it's your customers, not your competitors, who have you—and your margins—by the throat.

An accurate and honest appraisal of strategy decay is a powerful antidote to denial. (See the sidebar "Anticipating Strategy Decay" for a list of diagnostic questions.) It is also the only way to know whether renewal is proceeding fast enough to fully offset the declining economic effectiveness of today's strategies.

Valuing Variety

Life is the most resilient thing on the planet. It has survived meteor showers, seismic upheavals, and radical climate shifts. And yet it does not plan, it does not forecast, and, except when manifested in human beings, it possesses no foresight. So what is the essential thing that life teaches us about resilience? Just this: Variety matters. Genetic variety, within and across species, is nature's insurance policy against the unexpected. A high degree of biological diversity ensures that no matter what particular future unfolds, there will be at least some organisms that are well-suited to the new circumstances.

Evolutionary biologists aren't the only ones who understand the value of variety. As any systems theorist will tell you, the larger the variety of actions available to a system, the larger the variety of perturbations it is able to accommodate. Put simply, if the range of strategic alternatives your company is exploring is significantly narrower than the breadth of change in the environment, your business is going to be a victim of turbulence. Resilience depends on variety.

Big companies are used to making big bets—Disney's theme park outside Paris, Motorola's satellite-phone venture Iridium, HP's acquisition of Compaq, and GM's gamble on hydrogen-powered cars are but a few examples. Sometimes these bets pay off; often they don't. When audacious strategies fail, companies often react by imposing draconian cost-cutting measures. But neither profligacy nor privation leads to resilience. Most companies would be better off if they made fewer billion-dollar bets and a whole lot more $10,000 or $20,000 bets—some of which will, in time, justify more substantial commitments. They should steer clear of grand, imperial strategies and devote themselves instead to launching a swarm of low-risk experiments, or, as our colleague Amy Muller calls them, stratlets.

The arithmetic is clear: It takes thousands of ideas to produce dozens of promising stratlets to yield a few outsize successes. Yet only a handful of companies have committed themselves to broad-based, small-scale strategic experimentation. Whirlpool is one. The world's leading manufacturer of domestic appliances, Whirlpool competes in an industry that is both cyclical and mature. Growth is a function of housing starts and product replacement cycles. Customers tend to repair rather than replace their old appliances, particularly in tough times. Megaretailers like Best Buy squeeze margins mercilessly. Customers exhibit little brand loyalty. The result is zero-sum competition, steadily declining real prices, and low growth. Not content with this sorry state of affairs, Dave Whitwam, Whirlpool's chairman, set out in 1999 to make innovation a core competence at the company. He knew the only way to counter the forces that threatened Whirlpool's growth and profitability was to generate a wide assortment of genuinely novel strategic options.

Over the subsequent three years, the company involved roughly 10,000 of its 65,000 employees in the search for breakthroughs. In training sessions and workshops, these employees generated some 7,000 ideas, which spawned 300 small-scale experiments. From this cornucopia came a stream of new products and businesses—from Gladiator Garage Works, a line of modular storage units designed to reduce garage clutter; to Briva, a sink that features a small, high-speed dishwasher; to Gator Pak, an all-in-one food and entertainment center designed for tailgate parties. (For more on Whirlpool's strategy for commercializing the Gladiator line, see "Innovating for Cash," HBR, September 2003.)

Having institutionalized its experimentation process, Whirlpool now actively manages a broad pipeline of ideas, experiments, and major projects from across the company. Senior executives pay close attention to a set of measures—an innovation dashboard—that tracks the number of ideas moving through the pipeline, the percentage of those ideas that are truly new, and the potential financial impact of each one. Whirlpool's leadership team is learning just how much variety it must engender at the front end of the pipeline, in terms of nascent ideas and first-stage experiments, to produce the earnings impact it's looking for at the back end.

Experiments should go beyond just products. While virtually every company has some type of new-product pipeline, few have a process for continually generating, launching, and tracking novel strategy experiments in the areas of pricing, distribution, advertising, and customer service. Instead, many companies have created innovation ghettos—incubators, venture funds, business development functions, and skunk works—to pursue ideas outside the core. Cut off from the resources, competencies, and customers of the main business, most of these units produce little in the way of shareholder wealth, and many simply wither away.

The isolation—and distrust—of strategic experimentation is a leftover from the industrial age, when variety was often seen as the enemy. A variance, whether from a quality standard, a production schedule, or a budget, was viewed as a bad thing—which it often was. But in many companies, the aversion to unplanned variability has metastasized into a general antipathy toward the nonconforming and the deviant. This infatuation with conformance severely hinders the quest for resilience.

Our experience suggests that a reasonably large company or business unit—having $5 billion to $10 billion in revenues, say—should generate at least 100 groundbreaking experiments every year, with each one absorbing between $10,000 and $20,000 in first-stage investment funds. Such variety need not come at the expense of focus. Starting in the mid-1990s, Nokia pursued a strategy defined by three clear goals—to "humanize" technology (via the user interface, product design, and aesthetics); to enable "virtual presence" (where the phone becomes an all-purpose messaging and data access device); and to deliver "seamless solutions" (by bundling infrastructure, software, and handsets in a total package for telecom operators). Each of these "strategy themes" spawned dozens of breakthrough projects.

It is a broadly shared sense of direction, rather than a tightly circumscribed definition of served market or an allegiance to one particular business model, that reins in superfluous variety.

Of course, most billion-dollar opportunities don't start out as sure things—they start out as highly debatable propositions. For example, who would have predicted, in December 1995, when eBay was only three months old, that the on-line auctioneer would have a market value of $27 billion in the spring of 2003—two years *after* the dot-com crash? Sure, eBay is an exception. Success is always an exception. To find those exceptions, you must gather and sort through hundreds of new strategic options and then test the promising ones through low-cost, well-designed experiments—building prototypes, running computer simulations, interviewing progressive customers, and the like. There is simply no other way to reconnoiter the future. Most experiments *will* fail. The issue is not how many times you fail, but the value of your successes when compared with your failures. What counts is how the portfolio performs, rather than whether any particular experiment pans out.

Liberating Resources

Facing up to denial and fostering new ideas are great first steps. But they'll get you nowhere if you can't free up the resources to support a broad array of strategy experiments within the core business. As every manager knows, reallocating resources is an intensely political process. Resilience requires, however, that it become less so.

Institutions falter when they invest too much in "what is" and too little in "what could be." There are many ways companies over-invest in the status quo: They devote too much marketing energy to existing customer segments while ignoring new ones; they pour too many development dollars into incremental product enhancements while underfunding breakthrough projects; they lavish resources on existing distribution channels while starving new go-to-market strategies. But whatever the manifestation, the root cause is always the same: Legacy strategies have powerful constituencies; embryonic strategies do not.

In most organizations, a manager's power correlates directly with the resources he or she controls—to lose resources is to lose stature and influence. Moreover, personal success often turns solely on the performance of one's own unit or program. It is hardly surprising, then, that unit executives and program managers typically resist any attempt to reallocate "their" capital and talent to new initiatives— no matter how attractive those new initiatives may be. Of course, it's unseemly to appear too parochial, so managers often hide their motives behind the facade of an ostensibly prudent business argument. New projects are deemed "untested," "risky," or a "diversion." If such ruses are successful, and they often are, those seeking resources for new strategic options are forced to meet a higher burden of proof than are those who want to allocate additional investment dollars to existing programs. Ironically, unit managers seldom have to defend the risk they are taking when they pour good money into a slowly decaying strategy or overfund an activity that is already producing diminishing returns.

The fact is, novelty implies nothing about risk. Risk is a function of uncertainty, multiplied by the size of one's financial exposure. Newness is a function of the extent to which an idea defies precedent and convention. The Starbucks debit card, which allows regular customers to purchase their daily fix of caffeine without fumbling through their pockets for cash, was undoubtedly an innovation for the quick-serve restaurant industry. Yet it's not at all clear that it was risky. The card offers customers a solid benefit, and it relies on proven technology. Indeed, it was an immediate hit. Within 60 days of its launch, convenience-minded customers had snapped up 2.3 million cards and provided Starbucks with a $32 million cash float.

A persistent failure to distinguish between new ideas and risky ideas reinforces companies' tendency to overinvest in the past. So too does the general reluctance of corporate executives to shift resources from one business unit to another. A detailed study of diversified companies by business professors Hyun-Han Shin and René Stulz found that the allocation of investment funds across business units was mostly uncorrelated with the relative attractiveness of investment opportunities within those units. Instead, a business unit's investment budget was largely a function of its own cash flow and, secondarily, the cash flow of the firm as a whole. It seems that top-level executives, removed as they are from day-to-day operations, find it difficult to form a well-grounded view of unit-level, or subunit-level, opportunities and are therefore wary of real-locating resources from one unit to another.

Now, we're not suggesting that a highly profitable and growing business should be looted to fund some dim-witted diversification scheme. Yet if a company systematically favors existing programs over new initiatives, if the forces of preservation regularly trounce the forces of experimentation, it will soon find itself overinvesting in moribund strategies and outdated programs. Allocational rigidities are the enemy of resilience.

Just as biology can teach us something about variety, markets can teach us something about what it takes to liberate resources from the prison of precedent. The evidence of the past century leaves little room for doubt: Market-based economies outperform those that are centrally planned. It's not that markets are infallible. Like human beings, they are vulnerable to mania and despair. But, on average, markets are better than hierarchies at getting the right resources behind the right opportunities at the right time. Unlike hierarchies, markets are apolitical and unsentimental; they don't care whose ox gets gored. The average company, though, operates more like a socialist state than an unfettered market. A hierarchy may be an effective mechanism for applying resources, but it is an imperfect device for allocating resources. Specifically, the market for capital and talent that exists within companies is a whole lot less efficient than the market for talent and capital that exists between companies.

In fact, a company can be operationally efficient and strategically inefficient. It can maximize the efficiency of its existing programs and processes and yet fail to find and fund the unconventional ideas and initiatives that might yield an even higher return. While companies have many ways of assessing operational efficiency, most firms are clueless when it comes to strategic efficiency. How can corporate leaders be sure that the current set of initiatives represents the highest value use of talent and capital if the company hasn't generated and examined a large population of alternatives? And how can executives be certain that the right resources are lined up behind the right opportunities if capital and talent aren't free to move to high-return projects or businesses? The simple answer is, they can't.

When there is a dearth of novel strategic options, or when allocational rigidities lock up talent and cash in existing programs and businesses, managers are allowed to "buy" resources at a discount, meaning that they don't have to compete for resources against a wide array of alternatives. Requiring that every project and business earn its cost of capital doesn't correct this anomaly. It is perfectly possible for a company to earn its cost of capital and still fail to put its capital and talent to the most valuable uses.

To be resilient, businesses must minimize their propensity to overfund legacy strategies. At one large company, top management took an important step in this direction by earmarking 10% of its $1 billion-a-year capital budget for projects that were truly innovative. To qualify, a project had to have the potential to substantially change customer expectations or industry economics. Moreover, the CEO announced his intention to increase this percentage over time. He reasoned that if divisional executives were not funding breakout projects, the company was never going to achieve breakout results. The risk of this approach was mitigated by a requirement that each division develop a broad portfolio of experiments, rather than bet on one big idea.

Freeing up cash is one thing. Getting it into the right hands is another. Consider, for a moment, the options facing a politically disenfranchised employee who hopes to win funding for a small-scale strategy experiment. One option is to push the idea up the chain of command to the point where it can be considered as part of the formal planning process. This requires four things: a boss who doesn't peremptorily reject the idea as eccentric or out of scope; an idea that is, at first blush, "big" enough to warrant senior management's attention; executives who are willing to divert funds from existing programs in favor of the unconventional idea; and an innovator who has the business acumen, charisma, and political cunning to make all this happen. That makes for long odds.

What the prospective innovator needs is a second option: access to many, many potential investors—analogous to the multitude of investors to which a company can appeal when it is seeking to raise funds. How might this be accomplished? In large organizations there are hundreds, perhaps thousands, of individuals who control a budget of some sort—from facilities managers to sales managers to customer service managers to office managers and beyond. Imagine if each of these individuals were a potential source of funding for internal innovators. Imagine that each could occasionally play the role of angel investor by providing seed funding for ideas aimed at transforming the core business in ways large and small. What if everyone who managed a budget were allowed to invest 1% or 3% or 5% of that budget in strategy experiments? Investors within a particular department or region could form syndicates to take on slightly bigger risks or diversify their investment portfolios. To the extent that a portfolio produced a positive return, in terms of new revenues or big cost savings, a small bonus would go back to those who had provided the funds and served as sponsors and mentors. Perhaps investors with the best track records would be given the chance to invest more of their budgets in breakout projects. Thus liberated, capital would flow to the most intriguing possibilities, unfettered by executives' protectionist tendencies.

When it comes to renewal, human skills are even more critical than cash. So if a market for capital is important, a market for talent is essential. Whatever their location, individuals throughout a company need to be aware of all the new projects that are looking for talent. Distance, across business unit boundaries or national borders, should not diminish this visibility. Employees need a simple way to nominate themselves for project teams. And if a project team is eager to hire a particular person, no barriers should stand in the way of a transfer. Indeed, the project team should have a substantial amount of freedom in negotiating the terms of any transfer. As long as the overall project risk is kept within bounds, it should be up to the team to decide how much to pay for talent.

Executives shouldn't be too worried about protecting employees from the downside of a failed project. Over time, the most highly sought-after employees will have the chance to work on multiple projects, spreading their personal risk. However, it is important to ensure that successful projects generate meaningful returns, both financial and professional, for those involved, and that dedication to the cause of experimentation is always positively recognized. But irrespective of the financial rewards, ambitious employees will soon discover that transformational projects typically offer transformational opportunities for personal growth.

Embracing Paradox

The final barrier to resilience is ideological. The modern corporation is a shrine to a single, 100-year-old ideal—optimization. From "scientific management" to "operations research" to "reengineering" to "enterprise resource planning" to "Six Sigma," the goal has never changed: Do more, better, faster, and cheaper. Make no mistake, the ideology of optimization, and its elaboration into values, metrics, and processes, has created enormous material wealth. The ability to produce millions of gadgets, handle millions of transactions, or deliver a service to millions of customers is one of the most impressive achievements of humankind. But it is no longer enough.

The creed of optimization is perfectly summed up by McDonald's in its famous slogan, "Billions Served." The problem comes when some of those billions want to be served something else, something different, something new. As an ideal, optimization is sufficient only as long as there's no fundamental change in what has to be optimized. But if you work for a record company that needs to find a profitable online business model, or for an airline struggling to outmaneuver Southwest, or for a hospital trying to deliver quality care despite drastic budget cuts, or for a department store chain getting pummeled by discount retailers, or for an impoverished school district intent on curbing its dropout rate, or for any other organization where more of the same is no longer enough, then optimization is a wholly inadequate ideal.

An accelerating pace of change demands an accelerating pace of strategic evolution, which can be achieved only if a company cares as much about resilience as it does about optimization. This is currently not the case. Oh sure, companies have been working to improve their operational resilience—their ability to respond to the ups and downs of the business cycle or to quickly rebalance their product mix—but few have committed themselves to systematically tackling the challenge of strategic resilience. Quite the opposite, in fact. In recent years, most companies have been in retrenchment mode, working to resize their cost bases to accommodate a deflationary economy and unprecedented competitive pressure. But retrenchment can't revitalize a moribund business model, and great execution can't reverse the process of strategy decay.

It's not that optimization is wrong; it's that it so seldom has to defend itself against an equally muscular rival. Diligence, focus, and exactitude are reinforced every day, in a hundred ways—through training programs, benchmarking, improvement routines, and measurement systems. But where is the reinforcement for strategic variety, wide-scale experimentation, and rapid resource redeployment? How have these ideals been instantiated in employee training, performance metrics, and management processes? Mostly, they haven't been. That's why the forces of optimization are so seldom interrupted in their slow march to irrelevance.

When you run to catch a cab, your heart rate accelerates—*automatically*. When you stand up in front of an audience to speak, your adrenal glands start pumping—*spontaneously*. When you catch sight of someone alluring, your pupils dilate—*reflexively*. Automatic, spontaneous, reflexive. These words describe the way your body's autonomic systems respond to changes in your circumstances. They do not describe the way large organizations respond to changes in their circumstances. Resilience will become something like an autonomic process only when companies dedicate as much energy to laying the groundwork for perpetual renewal as they have to building the foundations for operational efficiency.

In struggling to embrace the inherent paradox between the relentless pursuit of efficiency and the restless exploration of new strategic options, managers can learn something from constitutional democracies, particularly the United States. Over more than two centuries, America has proven itself to be far more resilient than the companies it has spawned. At the heart of the American experiment is a paradox—unity and diversity—a single nation peopled by all nations. To be sure, it's not easy to steer a course between divisive sectarianism and totalitarian conformity. But the fact that America has managed to do this, despite some sad lapses, should give courage to managers trying to square the demands of penny-pinching efficiency and break-the-rules innovation. Maybe, just maybe, all those accountants and engineers, never great fans of paradox, can learn to love the heretics and the dreamers.

The Ultimate Advantage

Perhaps there are still some who believe that large organizations can never be truly resilient, that the goal of "zero trauma" is nothing more than a chimera. We believe they are wrong. Yes, size often shelters a company from the need to confront harsh truths. But why can't size also provide a shelter for new ideas? Size often confers an inappropriate sense of invincibility that leads to foolhardy risk-taking. But why can't size also confer a sense of possibility that encourages widespread experimentation? Size often implies inertia, but why can't it also imply persistence? The problem isn't size, but success. Companies get big because they do well. Size is a barrier to resilience only if those who inhabit large organizations fall prey to the delusion that success is self-perpetuating.

Battlefield commanders talk about "getting inside the enemy's decision cycle." If you can retrieve, interpret, and act upon battlefield intelligence faster than your adversary, they contend, you will be perpetually on the offensive, acting rather than reacting. In an analogous way, one can think about getting inside a competitor's "renewal cycle." Any company that can make sense of its environment, generate strategic options, and realign its resources faster than its rivals will enjoy a decisive advantage. This is the essence of resilience. And it will prove to be the ultimate competitive advantage in the age of turbulence—when companies are being challenged to change more profoundly, and more rapidly, than ever before.

Originally published in September 2003. Reprint R0309C

Disruptive Technologies

Catching the Wave. *by Joseph L. Bower and Clayton M. Christensen*

ONE OF THE MOST consistent patterns in business is the failure of leading companies to stay at the top of their industries when technologies or markets change. Goodyear and Firestone entered the radial-tire market quite late. Xerox let Canon create the small-copier market. Bucyrus-Erie allowed Caterpillar and Deere to take over the mechanical excavator market. Sears gave way to Wal-Mart.

The pattern of failure has been especially striking in the computer industry. IBM dominated the mainframe market but missed by years the emergence of minicomputers, which were technologically much simpler than mainframes. Digital Equipment dominated the minicomputer market with innovations like its VAX architecture but missed the personal-computer market almost completely. Apple Computer led the world of personal computing and established the standard for user-friendly computing but lagged five years behind the leaders in bringing its portable computer to market.

Why is it that companies like these invest aggressively—and successfully—in the technologies necessary to retain their current customers but then fail to make certain other technological investments that customers of the future will demand? Undoubtedly, bureaucracy, arrogance, tired executive blood, poor planning, and short-term investment horizons have all played a role. But a more fundamental reason lies at the heart of the paradox: leading companies succumb to one of the most popular, and valuable, management dogmas. They stay close to their customers.

Although most managers like to think they are in control, customers wield extraordinary power in directing a company's investments. Before managers decide to launch a technology, develop a product, build a plant, or establish new channels of distribution, they must look to their customers first: Do their customers want it? How big will the market be? Will the investment be profitable? The more astutely managers ask and answer these questions, the more completely their investments will be aligned with the needs of their customers.

This is the way a well-managed company should operate. Right? But what happens when customers reject a new technology, product concept, or way of doing business because it does *not* address their needs as effectively as a company's current approach? The large photocopying centers that represented the core of Xerox's customer base at first had no use for small, slow tabletop copiers. The excavation contractors that had relied on Bucyrus-Erie's big-bucket steam- and diesel-powered cable shovels didn't want hydraulic excavators because initially they were small and weak. IBM's large commercial, government, and industrial customers saw no immediate use for minicomputers. In each instance, companies listened to their customers, gave them the product performance they were looking for, and, in the end, were hurt by the very technologies their customers led them to ignore.

We have seen this pattern repeatedly in an ongoing study of leading companies in a variety of industries that have confronted technological change. The research shows that most well-managed, established companies are consistently ahead of their industries in developing and commercializing new technologies—from incremental improvements to radically new approaches—as long as those technologies address the next-generation performance needs of their customers. However, these same companies are rarely in the forefront of commercializing new technologies that don't initially meet the needs of mainstream customers and appeal only to small or emerging markets.

Idea in Brief

Goodyear, Xerox, Bucyrus-Erie, Digital. Leading companies all—yet they all failed to stay at the top of their industries when technologies or markets changed radically. That's disturbing enough, but the reason for the failure is downright alarming. The very processes that successful, well-managed companies use to serve the rapidly growing needs of their current customers can leave them highly vulnerable when market-changing technologies appear.

When a technology that has the potential for revolutionizing an industry emerges, established companies typically see it as unattractive: it's not something their mainstream customers want, and its projected profit margins aren't sufficient to cover big-company cost structures. As a result, the new technology tends to get ignored in favor of what's currently popular with the best customers. But then another company steps in to bring the innovation to a new market. Once the disruptive technology becomes established there, smaller-scale innovations rapidly raise the technology's performance on attributes that *mainstream* customers value.

What happens next is akin to the rapid, final moves leading to checkmate. The new technology invades the established market. By the time the established supplier—with its high overhead and profit margin requirements—wakes up and smells the coffee, its competitive disadvantage is insurmountable.

Using the rational, analytical investment processes that most well-managed companies have developed, it is nearly impossible to build a cogent case for diverting resources from known customer needs in established markets to markets and customers that seem insignificant or do not yet exist. After all, meeting the needs of established customers and fending off competitors takes all the resources a company has, and then some. In well-managed companies, the processes used to identify customers' needs, forecast technological trends, assess profitability, allocate resources across competing proposals for investment, and take new products to market are focused—for all the right reasons—on current customers and markets. These processes are designed to weed out proposed products and technologies that do *not* address customers' needs.

Idea in Practice

At issue here is a key distinction:

- **Sustaining innovation** maintains a steady rate of product improvement.

- **Disruptive innovation** often sacrifices performance along dimensions that are important to current customers and offers a very different package of attributes that are not (yet) valued by those customers. At the same time, the new attributes can open up entirely new markets. For example, Sony's early transistor radios sacrificed sound fidelity, but they created a new market for small, portable radios.

Staying focused on your main customers can work so well that you overlook disruptive technologies. The consequences can be far more disastrous than a missed opportunity. Case in point: not one of the independent hard-disk drive companies that existed in 1976 is still around today.

To prevent disruptive technologies from slipping through their fingers, established organizations must learn how to identify and nurture innovations on a more modest scale—so that small orders are meaningful, ill-defined markets have time to mature, and overhead is low enough to permit

In fact, the processes and incentives that companies use to keep focused on their main customers work so well that they blind those companies to important new technologies in emerging markets. Many companies have learned the hard way the perils of ignoring new technologies that do not initially meet the needs of mainstream customers. For example, although personal computers did not meet the requirements of mainstream minicomputer users in the early 1980s, the computing power of the desktop machines improved at a much faster rate than minicomputer users' *demands* for computing power did. As a result, personal computers caught up with the computing needs of many of the customers of Wang, Prime, Nixdorf, Data General, and Digital Equipment. Today they are performance-competitive with minicomputers in many applications. For the minicomputer makers, keeping close to mainstream customers and ignoring what were initially low-performance desktop technologies used by seemingly insignificant customers in emerging markets was a rational decision—but one that proved disastrous.

early profits. Here's a four-step guide:

1. **Determine whether the technology is disruptive or sustaining.** Ask the technical folks—they're more attuned than marketing and financial managers to which technologies have the potential to revolutionize the market.

2. **Define the strategic significance of the disruptive technology.** Your best customers are the last people to ask about this—sustaining technologies are what they care about.

3. **Locate the initial market for the disruptive technology.** If the market doesn't yet exist, conventional market research won't give you the information you need. So create it instead, by experimenting rapidly, iteratively, and inexpensively—with both the product and the market.

4. **House the disruptive technology in an independent entity.** For a disruptive technology to thrive, it can't be required to compete with established products for company resources.

The technological changes that damage established companies are usually not radically new or difficult from a *technological* point of view. They do, however, have two important characteristics: First, they typically present a different package of performance attributes—ones that, at least at the outset, are not valued by existing customers. Second, the performance attributes that existing customers do value improve at such a rapid rate that the new technology can later invade those established markets. Only at this point will mainstream customers want the technology. Unfortunately for the established suppliers, by then it is often too late: the pioneers of the new technology dominate the market.

It follows, then, that senior executives must first be able to spot the technologies that seem to fall into this category. Next, to commercialize and develop the new technologies, managers must protect them from the processes and incentives that are geared to serving established customers. And the only way to protect them is to create organizations that are completely independent from the mainstream business.

No industry demonstrates the danger of staying too close to customers more dramatically than the hard-disk-drive industry. Between 1976 and 1992, disk-drive performance improved at a stunning rate: the physical size of a 100-megabyte (MB) system shrank from 5,400 to 8 cubic inches, and the cost per MB fell from $560 to $5. Technological change, of course, drove these breathtaking achievements. About half of the improvement came from a host of radical advances that were critical to continued improvements in disk-drive performance; the other half came from incremental advances.

The pattern in the disk-drive industry has been repeated in many other industries: the leading, established companies have consistently led the industry in developing and adopting new technologies that their customers demanded—even when those technologies required completely different technological competencies and manufacturing capabilities from the ones the companies had. In spite of this aggressive technological posture, no single disk-drive manufacturer has been able to dominate the industry for more than a few years. A series of companies have entered the business and risen to prominence, only to be toppled by newcomers who pursued technologies that at first did not meet the needs of mainstream customers. As a result, not one of the independent disk-drive companies that existed in 1976 survives today.

To explain the differences in the impact of certain kinds of technological innovations on a given industry, the concept of *performance trajectories*—the rate at which the performance of a product has improved, and is expected to improve, over time—can be helpful. Almost every industry has a critical performance trajectory. In mechanical excavators, the critical trajectory is the annual improvement in cubic yards of earth moved per minute. In photocopiers, an important performance trajectory is improvement in number of copies per minute. In disk drives, one crucial measure of performance is storage capacity, which has advanced 50% each year on average for a given size of drive.

Different types of technological innovations affect performance trajectories in different ways. On the one hand, *sustaining* technologies tend to maintain a rate of improvement; that is, they give customers something more or better in the attributes they already value. For example, thin-film components in disk drives, which replaced conventional ferrite heads and oxide disks between 1982 and 1990, enabled information to be recorded more densely on disks. Engineers had been pushing the limits of the performance they could wring from ferrite heads and oxide disks, but the drives employing these technologies seemed to have reached the natural limits of an *S* curve. At that point, new thin-film technologies emerged that restored—or sustained—the historical trajectory of performance improvement.

On the other hand, *disruptive* technologies introduce a very different package of attributes from the one mainstream customers historically value, and they often perform far worse along one or two dimensions that are particularly important to those customers. As a rule, mainstream customers are unwilling to use a disruptive product in applications they know and understand. At first, then, disruptive technologies tend to be used and valued only in new markets or new applications; in fact, they generally make possible the emergence of new markets. For example, Sony's early transistor radios sacrificed sound fidelity but created a market for portable radios by offering a new and different package of attributes—small size, light weight, and portability.

In the history of the hard-disk-drive industry, the leaders stumbled at each point of disruptive technological change: when the diameter of disk drives shrank from the original 14 inches to 8 inches, then to 5.25 inches, and finally to 3.5 inches. Each of these new architectures initially offered the market substantially less storage capacity than the typical user in the established market required. For example, the 8-inch drive offered 20 MB when it was introduced, while the primary market for disk drives at that time—mainframes—required 200 MB on average. Not surprisingly, the leading computer manufacturers rejected the 8-inch architecture at first. As a result, their suppliers, whose mainstream products consisted of 14-inch drives with more than 200 MB of capacity, did not pursue the disruptive products aggressively. The pattern was repeated when the 5.25-inch and 3.5-inch drives emerged: established computer makers rejected the drives as inadequate, and, in turn, their disk-drive suppliers ignored them as well.

But while they offered less storage capacity, the disruptive architectures created other important attributes—internal power supplies and smaller size (8-inch drives); still smaller size and low-cost stepper motors (5.25-inch drives); and ruggedness, light weight, and low-power consumption (3.5-inch drives). From the late 1970s to the mid-1980s, the availability of the three drives made possible the development of new markets for minicomputers, desktop PCs, and portable computers, respectively.

Although the smaller drives represented disruptive technological change, each was technologically straightforward. In fact, there were engineers at many leading companies who championed the new technologies and built working prototypes with bootlegged resources before management gave a formal go-ahead. Still, the leading companies could not move the products through their organizations and into the market in a timely way. Each time a disruptive technology emerged, between one-half and two-thirds of the established manufacturers failed to introduce models employing the new architecture—in stark contrast to their timely launches of critical sustaining technologies. Those companies that finally did launch new models typically lagged behind entrant companies by two years—eons in an industry whose products' life cycles are often two years. Three waves of entrant companies led these revolutions; they first captured the new markets and then dethroned the leading companies in the mainstream markets.

How could technologies that were initially inferior and useful only to new markets eventually threaten leading companies in established markets? Once the disruptive architectures became established in their new markets, sustaining innovations raised each architecture's performance along steep trajectories—so steep that the performance available from each architecture soon satisfied the needs of customers in the established markets. For example, the 5.25-inch drive, whose initial 5 MB of capacity in 1980 was only a fraction of the capacity that the minicomputer market needed, became fully performance-competitive in the minicomputer market

How disk-drive performance met market needs

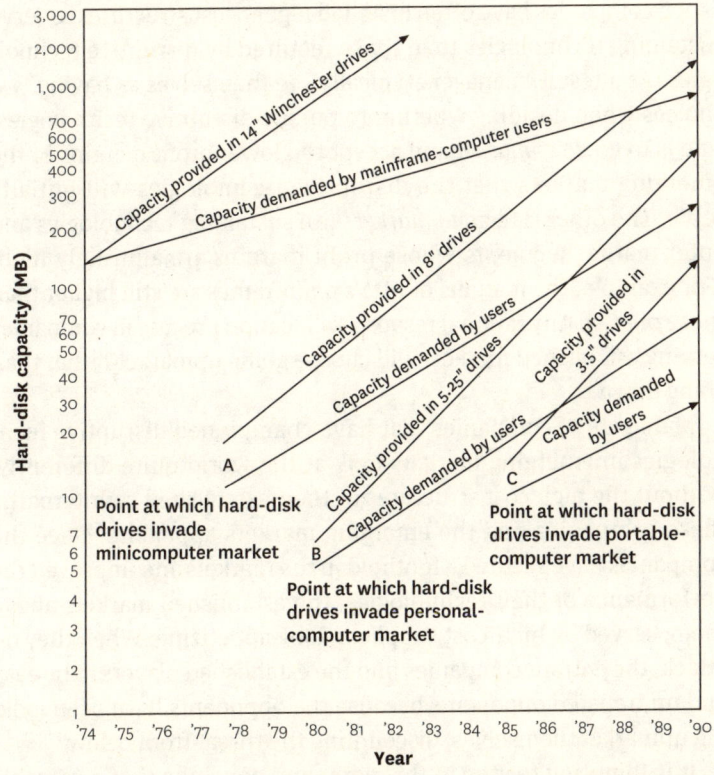

by 1986 and in the mainframe market by 1991. (See the graph "How disk-drive performance met market needs.")

A company's revenue and cost structures play a critical role in the way it evaluates proposed technological innovations. Generally, disruptive technologies look financially unattractive to established companies. The potential revenues from the discernible markets are small, and it is often difficult to project how big the markets for the technology will be over the long term. As a result, managers typically conclude that the technology cannot make a meaningful contribution to corporate growth and, therefore, that it is not worth the management effort required to develop it. In addition, established companies have often installed higher cost structures to serve sustaining technologies than those required by disruptive technologies. As a result, managers typically see themselves as having two choices when deciding whether to pursue disruptive technologies. One is to go *downmarket* and accept the lower profit margins of the emerging markets that the disruptive technologies will initially serve. The other is to go *upmarket* with sustaining technologies and enter market segments whose profit margins are alluringly high. (For example, the margins of IBM's mainframes are still higher than those of PCs). Any rational resource-allocation process in companies serving established markets will choose going upmarket rather than going down.

Managers of companies that have championed disruptive technologies in emerging markets look at the world quite differently. Without the high cost structures of their established counterparts, these companies find the emerging markets appealing. Once the companies have secured a foothold in the markets and improved the performance of their technologies, the established markets above them, served by high-cost suppliers, look appetizing. When they do attack, the entrant companies find the established players to be easy and unprepared opponents because the opponents have been looking upmarket themselves, discounting the threat from below.

It is tempting to stop at this point and conclude that a valuable lesson has been learned: managers can avoid missing the next wave by paying careful attention to potentially disruptive technologies that do *not* meet current customers' needs. But recognizing the pattern and figuring out how to break it are two different things. Although entrants invaded established markets with new technologies three times in succession, none of the established leaders in the disk-drive industry seemed to learn from the experiences of those that fell before them. Management myopia or lack of foresight cannot explain these failures. The problem is that managers keep doing what has worked in the past: serving the rapidly growing needs of their current customers. The processes that successful, well-managed companies have developed to allocate resources among proposed investments are *incapable* of funneling resources into programs that current customers explicitly don't want and whose profit margins seem unattractive.

Managing the development of new technology is tightly linked to a company's investment processes. Most strategic proposals—to add capacity or to develop new products or processes—take shape at the lower levels of organizations in engineering groups or project teams. Companies then use analytical planning and budgeting systems to select from among the candidates competing for funds. Proposals to create new businesses in emerging markets are particularly challenging to assess because they depend on notoriously unreliable estimates of market size. Because managers are evaluated on their ability to place the right bets, it is not surprising that in well-managed companies, mid- and top-level managers back projects in which the market seems assured. By staying close to lead customers, as they have been trained to do, managers focus resources on fulfilling the requirements of those reliable customers that can be served profitably. Risk is reduced—and careers are safeguarded—by giving known customers what they want.

Seagate Technology's experience illustrates the consequences of relying on such resource-allocation processes to evaluate disruptive technologies. By almost any measure, Seagate, based in Scotts Valley, California, was one of the most successful and aggressively managed companies in the history of the microelectronics industry: From its inception in 1980, Seagate's revenues had grown to more than $700 million by 1986. It had pioneered 5.25-inch hard-disk drives and was the main supplier of them to IBM and IBM-compatible personal-computer manufacturers. The company was the leading manufacturer of 5.25-inch drives at the time the disruptive 3.5-inch drives emerged in the mid-1980s.

Engineers at Seagate were the second in the industry to develop working prototypes of 3.5-inch drives. By early 1985, they had made more than 80 such models with a low level of company funding. The engineers forwarded the new models to key marketing executives, and the trade press reported that Seagate was actively developing 3.5-inch drives. But Seagate's principal customers—IBM and other manufacturers of AT-class personal computers—showed no interest in the new drives. They wanted to incorporate 40-MB and 60-MB drives in their next-generation models, and Seagate's early 3.5-inch prototypes packed only 10 MB. In response, Seagate's marketing executives lowered their sales forecasts for the new disk drives.

Manufacturing and financial executives at the company pointed out another drawback to the 3.5-inch drives. According to their analysis, the new drives would never be competitive with the 5.25-inch architecture on a cost-per-megabyte basis—an important metric that Seagate's customers used to evaluate disk drives. Given Seagate's cost structure, margins on the higher-capacity 5.25-inch models therefore promised to be much higher than those on the smaller products.

Senior managers quite rationally decided that the 3.5-inch drive would not provide the sales volume and profit margins that Seagate needed from a new product. A former Seagate marketing executive recalled, "We needed a new model that could become the next ST412 [a 5.25-inch drive generating more than $300 million in annual sales, which was nearing the end of its life cycle]. At the time, the entire market for 3.5-inch drives was less than $50 million. The 3.5-inch drive just didn't fit the bill—for sales or profits."

The shelving of the 3.5-inch drive was *not* a signal that Seagate was complacent about innovation. Seagate subsequently introduced new models of 5.25-inch drives at an accelerated rate and, in so doing, introduced an impressive array of sustaining technological improvements, even though introducing them rendered a significant portion of its manufacturing capacity obsolete.

While Seagate's attention was glued to the personal-computer market, former employees of Seagate and other 5.25-inch drive makers, who had become frustrated by their employers' delays in launching 3.5-inch drives, founded a new company, Conner Peripherals. Conner focused on selling its 3.5-inch drives to companies in emerging markets for portable computers and small-footprint desktop products (PCs that take up a smaller amount of space on a desk).

Conner's primary customer was Compaq Computer, a customer that Seagate had never served. Seagate's own prosperity, coupled with Conner's focus on customers who valued different disk-drive attributes (ruggedness, physical volume, and weight), minimized the threat Seagate saw in Conner and its 3.5-inch drives.

From its beachhead in the emerging market for portable computers, however, Conner improved the storage capacity of its drives by 50% per year. By the end of 1987, 3.5-inch drives packed the capacity demanded in the mainstream personal-computer market. At this point, Seagate executives took their company's 3.5-inch drive off the shelf, introducing it to the market as a *defensive* response to the attack of entrant companies like Conner and Quantum Corporation, the other pioneer of 3.5-inch drives. But it was too late.

By then, Seagate faced strong competition. For a while, the company was able to defend its existing market by selling 3.5-inch drives to its established customer base—manufacturers and resellers of full-size personal computers. In fact, a large proportion of its 3.5-inch products continued to be shipped in frames that enabled its customers to mount the drives in computers designed to accommodate 5.25-inch drives. But, in the end, Seagate could only struggle to become a second-tier supplier in the new portable-computer market.

In contrast, Conner and Quantum built a dominant position in the new portable-computer market and then used their scale and experience base in designing and manufacturing 3.5-inch products to drive Seagate from the personal-computer market. In their 1994 fiscal years, the combined revenues of Conner and Quantum exceeded $5 billion.

Seagate's poor timing typifies the responses of many established companies to the emergence of disruptive technologies. Seagate was willing to enter the market for 3.5-inch drives only when it had become large enough to satisfy the company's financial requirements—that is, only when existing customers wanted the new technology. Seagate has survived through its savvy acquisition of Control Data Corporation's disk-drive business in 1990. With CDC's technology base and Seagate's volumemanufacturing expertise, the company has become a powerful player in the business of supplying large-capacity drives for high-end computers. Nonetheless, Seagate has been reduced to a shadow of its former self in the personal-computer market.

It should come as no surprise that few companies, when confronted with disruptive technologies, have been able to overcome the handicaps of size or success. But it can be done. There is a method to spotting and cultivating disruptive technologies.

Determine whether the technology is disruptive or sustaining

The first step is to decide which of the myriad technologies on the horizon are disruptive and, of those, which are real threats. Most companies have well-conceived processes for identifying and tracking the progress of potentially sustaining technologies, because they are important to serving and protecting current customers. But few have systematic processes in place to identify and track potentially disruptive technologies.

One approach to identifying disruptive technologies is to examine internal disagreements over the development of new products or technologies. Who supports the project and who doesn't? Marketing and financial managers, because of their managerial and financial incentives, will rarely support a disruptive technology. On the other hand, technical personnel with outstanding track records will often persist in arguing that a new market for the technology will emerge—even in the face of opposition from key customers and marketing and financial staff. Disagreement between the two groups often signals a disruptive technology that top-level managers should explore.

Define the strategic significance of the disruptive technology

The next step is to ask the right people the right questions about the strategic importance of the disruptive technology. Disruptive technologies tend to stall early in strategic reviews because managers either ask the wrong questions or ask the wrong people the right questions. For example, established companies have regular procedures for asking mainstream customers—especially the important accounts where new ideas are actually tested—to assess the value of innovative products. Generally, these customers are selected because they are the ones striving the hardest to stay ahead of *their* competitors in pushing the performance of *their* products. Hence these customers are most likely to demand the highest performance from their suppliers. For this reason, lead customers are reliably accurate when it comes to assessing the potential of sustaining technologies, but they are reliably *in*accurate when it comes to assessing the potential of disruptive technologies. They are the wrong people to ask.

A simple graph plotting product performance as it is defined in mainstream markets on the vertical axis and time on the horizontal axis can help managers identify both the right questions and the right people to ask. First, draw a line depicting the level of performance and the trajectory of performance improvement that customers have historically enjoyed and are likely to expect in the future. Then locate the estimated initial performance level of the new technology. If the technology is disruptive, the point will lie far below the performance demanded by current customers. (See the graph "How to assess disruptive technologies.")

What is the likely slope of performance improvement of the disruptive technology compared with the slope of performance improvement demanded by existing markets? If knowledgeable technologists believe the new technology might progress faster than the market's demand for performance improvement, then that technology, which does not meet customers' needs today, may very well address them tomorrow. The new technology, therefore, is strategically critical.

Instead of taking this approach, most managers ask the wrong questions. They compare the anticipated rate of performance improvement of the new technology with that of the established technology. If the new technology has the potential to surpass the established one, the reasoning goes, they should get busy developing it.

Pretty simple. But this sort of comparison, while valid for sustaining technologies, misses the central strategic issue in assessing potentially disruptive technologies. Many of the disruptive technologies we studied *never* surpassed the capability of the old technology. It is the trajectory of the disruptive technology compared with that of the *market* that is significant. For example, the reason the mainframe-computer market is shrinking is not that personal computers outperform mainframes but because personal computers networked with a file server meet the computing and datastorage needs of many organizations effectively. Mainframe-computer makers are reeling not because the performance of personalcomputing technology surpassed the performance of mainframe *technology* but because it intersected with the performance demanded by the established *market*.

Consider the graph again. If technologists believe that the new technology will progress at the same rate as the market's demand for performance improvement, the disruptive technology may be slower to invade established markets. Recall that Seagate had targeted personal computing, where demand for hard-disk capacity per computer was growing at 30% per year. Because the capacity of 3.5-inch drives improved at a much faster rate, leading 3.5-inch-drive makers were able to force Seagate out of the market. However, two other 5.25-inch-drive makers, Maxtor and Micropolis, had targeted the engineering-workstation market, in which demand for hard-disk capacity was insatiable. In that market, the trajectory of capacity

How to assess disruptive technologies

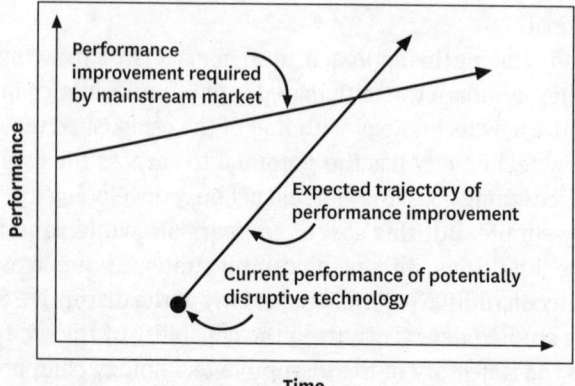

demanded was essentially parallel to the trajectory of capacity improvement that technologists could supply in the 3.5-inch architecture. As a result, entering the 3.5-inch-drive business was strategically less critical for those companies than it was for Seagate.

Locate the initial market for the disruptive technology

Once managers have determined that a new technology is disruptive and strategically critical, the next step is to locate the initial markets for that technology. Market research, the tool that managers have traditionally relied on, is seldom helpful: at the point a company needs to make a strategic commitment to a disruptive technology, no concrete market exists. When Edwin Land asked Polaroid's market researchers to assess the potential sales of his new camera, they concluded that Polaroid would sell a mere 100,000 cameras over the product's lifetime; few people they interviewed could imagine the uses of instant photography.

Because disruptive technologies frequently signal the emergence of new markets or market segments, managers must *create* information about such markets—who the customers will be, which dimensions of product performance will matter most to which customers, what the right price points will be. Managers can create this kind of information only by experimenting rapidly, iteratively, and inexpensively with both the product and the market.

For established companies to undertake such experiments is very difficult. The resource-allocation processes that are critical to profitability and competitiveness will not—and should not—direct resources to markets in which sales will be relatively small. How, then, can an established company probe a market for a disruptive technology? Let startups—either ones the company funds or others with no connection to the company—conduct the experiments. Small, hungry organizations are good at placing economical bets, rolling with the punches, and agilely changing product and market strategies in response to feedback from initial forays into the market.

Consider Apple Computer in its startup days. The company's original product, the Apple I, was a flop when it was launched in 1977. But Apple had not placed a huge bet on the product and had gotten at least *something* into the hands of early users quickly. The company learned a lot from the Apple I about the new technology and about what customers wanted and did not want. Just as important, a group of *customers* learned about what they did and did not want from personal computers. Armed with this information, Apple launched the Apple II quite successfully.

Many companies could have learned the same valuable lessons by watching Apple closely. In fact, some companies pursue an explicit strategy of being *second to invent*—allowing small pioneers to lead the way into uncharted market territory. For instance, IBM let Apple, Commodore, and Tandy define the personal computer. It then aggressively entered the market and built a considerable personal-computer business.

But IBM's relative success in entering a new market late is the exception, not the rule. All too often, successful companies hold the performance of small-market pioneers to the financial standards they apply to their own performance. In an attempt to ensure that they are using their resources well, companies explicitly or implicitly set relatively high thresholds for the size of the markets they should consider entering. This approach sentences them to making late entries into markets already filled with powerful players.

For example, when the 3.5-inch drive emerged, Seagate needed a $300-million-a-year product to replace its mature flagship 5.25-inch model, the ST412, and the 3.5-inch market wasn't large enough. Over the next two years, when the trade press asked when Seagate would introduce its 3.5-inch drive, company executives consistently responded that there was no market yet. There actually *was* a market, and it was growing rapidly. The signals that Seagate was picking up about the market, influenced as they were by customers who didn't want 3.5-inch drives, were misleading. When Seagate finally introduced its 3.5-inch drive in 1987, more than $750 million in 3.5-inch drives had already been sold. Information about the market's size had been widely available throughout the industry. But it wasn't compelling enough to shift the focus of Seagate's managers. They continued to look at the new market through the eyes of their current customers and in the context of their current financial structure.

The posture of today's leading disk-drive makers toward the newest disruptive technology, 1.8-inch drives, is eerily familiar. Each of the industry leaders has designed one or more models of the tiny drives, and the models are sitting on shelves. Their capacity is too low to be used in notebook computers, and no one yet knows where the initial market for 1.8-inch drives will be. Fax machines, printers, and automobile dashboard mapping systems are all candidates. "There just isn't a market," complained one industry executive. "We've got the product, and the sales force can take orders for it. But there are no orders because nobody needs it. It just sits there." This executive has not considered the fact that his sales force has no incentive to sell the 1.8-inch drives instead of the higher-margin products it sells to higher-volume customers. And while the 1.8-inch drive is sitting on the shelf at his company and others, last year more than $50 million worth of 1.8-inch drives were sold, almost all by startups. This year, the market will be an estimated $150 million.

To avoid allowing small, pioneering companies to dominate new markets, executives must personally monitor the available intelligence on the progress of pioneering companies through monthly meetings with technologists, academics, venture capitalists, and other nontraditional sources of information. They *cannot* rely on the company's traditional channels for gauging markets because those channels were not designed for that purpose.

Place responsibility for building a disruptive-technology business in an independent organization

The strategy of forming small teams into skunk-works projects to isolate them from the stifling demands of mainstream organizations is widely known but poorly understood. For example, isolating a team of engineers so that it can develop a radically new sustaining technology just because that technology is radically different is a fundamental misapplication of the skunkworks approach. Managing out of context is also unnecessary in the unusual event that a disruptive technology is more financially attractive than existing products. Consider Intel's transition from dynamic random access memory (DRAM) chips to microprocessors. Intel's early microprocessor business had a higher gross margin than that of its DRAM business; in other words, Intel's normal resource-allocation process naturally provided the new business with the resources it needed.[1]

Creating a separate organization is necessary only when the disruptive technology has a lower profit margin than the mainstream business and must serve the unique needs of a new set of customers. CDC, for example, successfully created a remote organization to commercialize its 5.25-inch drive. Through 1980, CDC was the dominant independent disk-drive supplier due to its expertise in making 14-inch drives for mainframe-computer makers. When the 8-inch drive emerged, CDC launched a late development effort, but its engineers were repeatedly pulled off the project to solve problems for the more profitable, higher-priority 14-inch projects targeted at the company's most important customers. As a result, CDC was three years late in launching its first 8-inch product and never captured more than 5% of that market.

When the 5.25-inch generation arrived, CDC decided that it would face the new challenge more strategically. The company assigned a small group of engineers and marketers in Oklahoma City, Oklahoma, far from the mainstream organization's customers, the task of developing and commercializing a competitive 5.25-inch product. "We needed to launch it in an environment in which everybody got excited about a $50,000 order," one executive recalled. "In Minneapolis, you needed a $1 million order to turn anyone's head." CDC never regained the 70% share it had once enjoyed in the market for mainframe disk drives, but its Oklahoma City operation secured a profitable 20% of the high-performance 5.25-inch market.

Had Apple created a similar organization to develop its Newton personal digital assistant (PDA), those who have pronounced it a flop might have deemed it a success. In launching the product, Apple made the mistake of acting as if it were dealing with an established market. Apple managers went into the PDA project assuming that it had to make a significant contribution to corporate growth. Accordingly, they researched customer desires exhaustively and then bet huge sums launching the Newton. Had Apple made a more modest technological and financial bet and entrusted the Newton to an organization the size that Apple itself was when it launched the

Apple I, the outcome might have been different. The Newton might have been seen more broadly as a solid step forward in the quest to discover what customers really want. In fact, many more Newtons than Apple I models were sold within a year of their introduction.

Keep the disruptive organization independent

Established companies can only dominate emerging markets by creating small organizations of the sort CDC created in Oklahoma City. But what should they do when the emerging market becomes large and established?

Most managers assume that once a spin-off has become commercially viable in a new market, it should be integrated into the mainstream organization. They reason that the fixed costs associated with engineering, manufacturing, sales, and distribution activities can be shared across a broader group of customers and products.

This approach might work with sustaining technologies; however, with disruptive technologies, folding the spin-off into the mainstream organization can be disastrous. When the independent and mainstream organizations are folded together in order to share resources, debilitating arguments inevitably arise over which groups get what resources and whether or when to cannibalize established products. In the history of the disk-drive industry, every company that has tried to manage mainstream and disruptive businesses within a single organization failed.

No matter the industry, a corporation consists of business units with finite life spans: the technological and market bases of any business will eventually disappear. Disruptive technologies are part of that cycle. Companies that understand this process can create new businesses to replace the ones that must inevitably die. To do so, companies must give managers of disruptive innovation free rein to realize the technology's full potential—even if it means ultimately killing the mainstream business. For the corporation to live, it must be willing to see business units die. If the corporation doesn't kill them off itself, competitors will.

The key to prospering at points of disruptive change is not simply to take more risks, invest for the long term, or fight bureaucracy. The key is to manage strategically important disruptive technologies in an organizational context where small orders create energy, where fast low-cost forays into ill-defined markets are possible, and where overhead is low enough to permit profit even in emerging markets.

Managers of established companies can master disruptive technologies with extraordinary success. But when they seek to develop and launch a disruptive technology that is rejected by important customers within the context of the mainstream business's financial demands, they fail—not because they make the wrong decisions, but because they make the right decisions for circumstances that are about to become history.

Originally published in January–February 1995. Reprint 95103

Organizational Grit

by Thomas H. Lee and Angela L. Duckworth

HIGH ACHIEVERS HAVE extraordinary stamina. Even if they're already at the top of their game, they're always striving to improve. Even if their work requires sacrifice, they remain in love with what they do. Even when easier paths beckon, their commitment is steadfast. We call this remarkable combination of strengths "grit."

Grit predicts who will accomplish challenging goals. Research done at West Point, for example, shows that it's a better indicator of which cadets will make it through training than achievement test scores and athletic ability. Grit predicts the likelihood of graduating from high school and college and performance in stressful jobs such as sales. Grit also, we believe, propels people to the highest ranks of leadership in many demanding fields.

In health care, patients have long depended on the grit of individual doctors and nurses. But in modern medicine, providing superior care has become so complex that no lone practitioner, no matter how driven, can do it all. Today great care requires great collaboration—gritty teams of clinicians who all relentlessly push for improvement. Yet it takes more than that: Health care institutions must exhibit grit across the entire provider system.

In this article, drawing on Tom's decades of experience as a clinician and health care leader and Angela's foundational studies on grit, we've integrated psychological research at the individual level with contemporary perspectives on organizational and health care cultures. As we'll show, in the new model of grit in health care—exemplified by leading institutions like Mayo Clinic and Cleveland

Clinic—passion for patient well-being and perseverance in the pursuit of that goal become social norms at the individual, team, and institutional levels. Health care, because it attracts so many elite performers and is so dependent on teamwork, is an exceptionally good place to find examples of organizational grit. But the principles outlined here can be applied in other business sectors as well.

Developing Individuals

For leaders, building a gritty culture begins with selecting and developing gritty individuals. What should organizations look for? The two critical components of grit are passion and perseverance. Passion comes from intrinsic interest in your craft and from a sense of purpose—the conviction that your work is meaningful and helps others. Perseverance takes the form of resilience in the face of adversity as well as unwavering devotion to continuous improvement.

The kind of single-minded determination that characterizes the grittiest individuals requires a clearly aligned hierarchy of goals. Consider what such a hierarchy might look like for a cardiologist: At the bottom would be specific tasks on her short-term to-do list, such as meetings to review cases. These low-level goals are a means to an end, helping the cardiologist accomplish mid-level goals, such as coordinating patients' care with other specialists and team members. At the top would be a goal that is abstract, broad, and important— such as increasing patients' quality and length of life. This overarching goal gives meaning and direction to everything a gritty individual does. (See the exhibit "A cardiologist's goal hierarchy.") Less gritty people, in contrast, have less coherent goal hierarchies—and often, numerous conflicts among goals at every level.

It's important to note that assembling a group of gritty people does not necessarily create a gritty organization. It could instead yield a disorganized crowd of driven individuals, each pursuing a separate passion. If everyone's goals aren't aligned, a culture won't be gritty. And, as we'll discuss in more detail later, it takes effort to achieve that alignment.

Idea in Brief

The Problem

Health care has long depended on the passion and perseverance of individual doctors and nurses. But with the advent of modern medicine, providing superior care has become so complex that no lone caregiver, no matter how gritty, can do it all.

The Solution

Hospitals and health systems must develop grit at the individual, team, and organizational levels. That requires ensuring that all participants are committed to pursuing a shared high-level goal. Putting patients first is a common and effective objective.

How It Works

Sustaining a gritty organizational culture requires clear communication of values by leadership, programs that celebrate successes, and the promotion of a "growth mindset" that embraces continuous improvement and learning from setbacks.

Take Mayo Clinic. It is unambivalently committed to a top-level goal of putting patients' needs above all else. It lays out that goal in its mission statement and diligently reinforces it when recruiting. Mayo observes outside job candidates for two to three days as they practice and teach, evaluating not just their skills but also their values—specifically, whether they have a patient-centric mission. Once hired, new doctors undergo a three-year evaluation period. Only after they've demonstrated the needed talent, grit, and goal alignment are they considered for permanent appointment.

How can you hire for grit? Questionnaires are useful for research and self-reflection (see the sidebar "Gauging Your Grit"), but because they're easy to game, we don't recommend using them as hiring tools. Instead, we recommend carefully reviewing an applicant's track record. In particular, look for multiyear commitments and objective evidence of advancement and achievement, as opposed to frequent lateral moves, such as shifts from one specialty to another. When checking references, listen for evidence that candidates have bounced back from failure in the past, demonstrated flexibility in dealing with unexpected obstacles, and sustained a habit of continuous self-improvement. Most of all, look for signs that people are

A cardiologist's goal hierarchy

In this simplified illustration, immediate, concrete goals sit at the bottom. These support broader goals at the next level, which in turn support an overarching primary goal that provides meaning and direction.

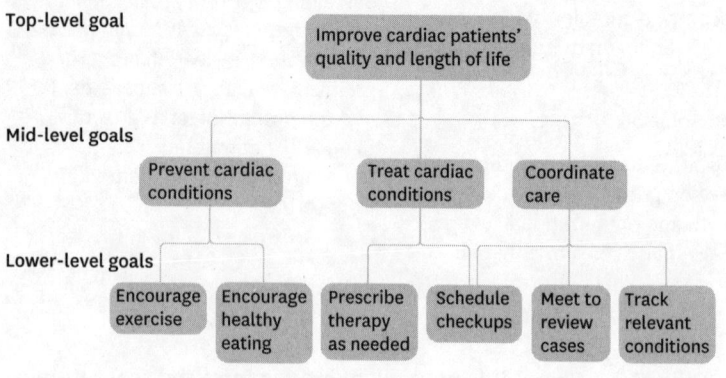

driven by a purpose bigger than themselves, one that resonates with the mission of your organization.

Mayo, like many gritty organizations, develops most of its own talent. More than half the physicians hired at its main campus in Rochester, Minnesota, for example, come from its medical school or training programs. One leader there told us those programs are seen as "an eight-year job interview." When expanding to other regions, both Mayo and Cleveland Clinic prefer to transfer physicians trained within their systems rather than hire local doctors who may not fit their culture.

Creating the right environment can help organizations develop employees with grit. (The idea of cultivating passion and perseverance in adults may seem naive, but abundant research shows that character continues to evolve over a lifetime.) The optimal environment will be both demanding and supportive. People will be asked to meet high expectations, which will be clearly defined and feasible though challenging. But they'll also be offered the psychological safety and trust, plus tangible resources, that they need to take risks, make mistakes, and keep learning and growing.

At Cleveland Clinic, physicians are on one-year contracts, which are renewed—or not—on the basis of their annual professional reviews (APRs). These include a formal discussion of career goals. Before an APR, each of the clinic's 3,600 physicians completes an online assessment, reflects on his or her progress over the past year, and proposes new objectives for the year ahead. At the meetings, physicians and their supervisors agree on specific goals, such as improving communication skills or learning new techniques. The clinic then offers relevant courses or training along with the financial support and "protected time" the physicians might need to complete it. Improvement is encouraged not by performance bonuses but by giving people detailed feedback about how they're doing on a host of metrics, including efficiency at specific procedures and patient experience. The underlying assumption is that clinicians want to improve and that the organization, and their supervisors in particular, fully backs their efforts to reach targets that may take a year or more to reach.

Building Teams

Gritty teams collectively have the same traits that gritty individuals do: a desire to work hard, learn, and improve; resilience in the face of setbacks; and a strong sense of priorities and purpose.

In health care, teams are often defined by the population they serve (say, patients with breast cancer) or the site where they work (the coronary care unit). Gritty team members may have their own professional goal hierarchies, but each will embrace the team's high-level goal—typically, a team-specific objective, such as "improve our breast cancer patients' outcomes," that in turn supports the organization's overarching goal.

Many people in health care associate commitment to a team with the loss of autonomy—a negative—but gritty people view it as an opportunity to provide better care for their patients. They see the whole as greater than the sum of its parts, recognizing that they can achieve more as a team than as individuals.

In business, teams are increasingly dispersed and virtual, but the grittiest health care teams we've seen emphasize face-to-face interaction. Members meet frequently to review cases, set targets for improvement, and track progress. In many instances the entire team discusses each new patient. These meetings reinforce the sense of shared purpose and commitment and help members get to know one another and build trust—another characteristic of effective teams.

That's an insight that many health care leaders have come to by studying the description of the legendary six-month Navy SEAL training in *Team of Teams,* by General Stanley McChrystal. As he notes, the training's purpose is "not to produce supersoldiers. It is to build superteams." He writes, "Few tasks are tackled alone . . . The formation of SEAL teams is less about preparing people to follow precise orders than it is about developing trust and the ability to adapt within a small group." Such a culture allows teams to perform at consistently high levels, even in the face of unpredictable challenges.

Commitment to a shared purpose, a focus on constant improvement, and mutual trust are all hallmarks of integrated practice units (IPUs)—the gold standard in team health care. These multidisciplinary units provide the full cycle of care for a group of patients, usually those with the same condition or closely related conditions. Because IPUs focus on well-defined segments of patients with similar needs, meaningful data can be collected on their costs and outcomes. That means that the value a unit creates can be measured, optimized, and rewarded. In other words, IPUs can gather the feedback they need to keep getting better.

UCLA's kidney transplant IPU is a prime example. Two years after the 1984 passage of the National Organ Transplant Act, which required organ transplant programs to collect and report data on outcomes such as one-year success rates, Kaiser Permanente approached UCLA about contracting for kidney transplantation. This dominant HMO would increase its referrals to UCLA if UCLA would accept a fixed price for the entire episode of care (a "bundled payment"). After taking the deal, UCLA had an imperative to deliver great outcomes (or risk public humiliation and loss of referrals) and be efficient (or risk losing money under the bundled payment contract).

The team has grown to be one of the largest in the country, and its success rates (risk-adjusted patient and graft survival) have been significantly higher than national benchmarks almost every year. With medical advances and public reporting, kidney transplantation success rates have improved across the country—but UCLA has stayed at the front of the pack.

Gritty Organizations

If gritty individuals and teams are to thrive, organizations need to develop cultures that make them, in turn, macrocosms of their best teams and people.

So organizations benefit from making their goal hierarchies explicit. If an organization declares that it has multiple missions, and can't prioritize them, it will have difficulty making good strategic choices.

Another danger is promoting a high-level objective that people won't embrace. In health care making cost cutting or growth in market share the top priority is unlikely to resonate with caregivers whose passion is improving outcomes that matter to patients.

In our experience, every gritty health care organization has a primary goal of putting patients first. In fact, we believe a health care organization can't be gritty if it doesn't put that goal before everything else. (See the exhibit "Aligning organizational objectives.") Though it's challenging to suggest that other needs (such as those of doctors or researchers) come second or third, if patients' needs are not foremost, decisions tend to be based on politics rather than strategy as stakeholders jockey for resources. This doesn't mean an organization can't have other goals; Mayo, for instance, also values research, education, and public health. But those things are subordinate to patient care.

Of course, even when the high-level goal is clear and appropriate, rhetoric alone won't suffice to promote it—and can even backfire. If an organization's leaders don't use the goal to make decisions, it will undermine their credibility.

Consider how Cleveland Clinic responded when it learned that a delayed appointment had caused hours of suffering for a patient

Aligning organizational objectives

Gritty health care institutions have clear goal hierarchies, like the hypothetical schematic below. As with individual and team hierarchies, lower-level goals support those at the next tier, in service of a single, overarching top-level goal or mission.

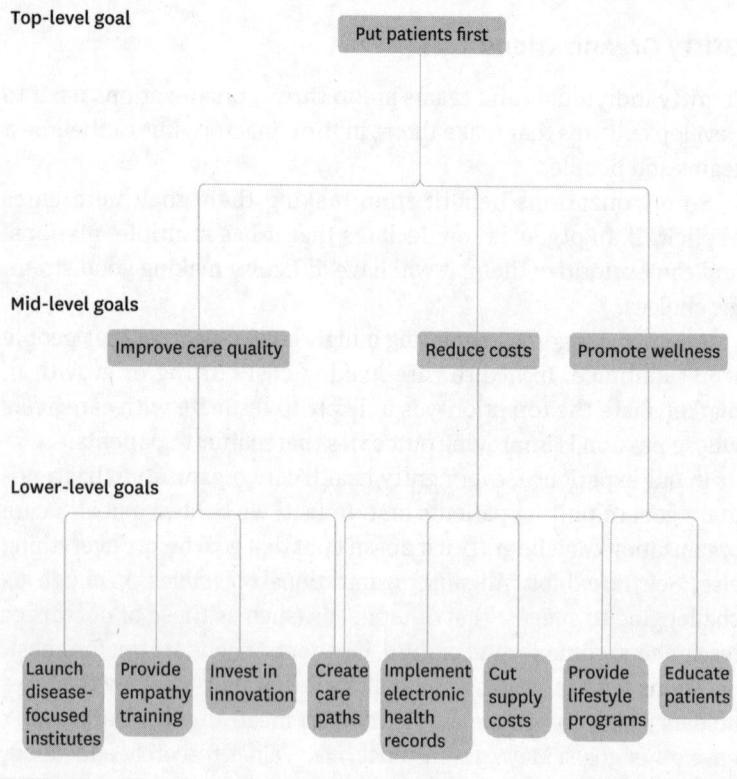

Top-level goal — Put patients first

Mid-level goals — Improve care quality | Reduce costs | Promote wellness

Lower-level goals — Launch disease-focused institutes | Provide empathy training | Invest in innovation | Create care paths | Implement electronic health records | Cut supply costs | Provide lifestyle programs | Educate patients

with difficulty urinating. The clinic began asking everyone requesting an appointment whether he or she wanted to be seen that day. Offering that option required complex and costly changes in how things were done, but it clearly put patients' needs first. As it happened, the change was rewarded with tremendous increases in market share, but this was a happy side effect, not the main intent of the change.

As this story shows, clarity around high-level goals can be a competitive differentiator in the market and have a valuable impact within the organization as well. Data from Press Ganey demonstrates that when clinicians and other employees embrace their organization's commitment to quality and safety, and when those goals reflect their own, it leads not only to better care but also to better business results.

But how can leaders help translate the top-level organizational goal into practical activities for teams and individuals? Seven years ago Cleveland Clinic took an important step that helped define its culture and direction. Toby Cosgrove, the CEO at the time, had all employees engage in a half-day "appreciative inquiry" program, in which personnel in various roles sat at tables of about 10 and discussed cases in which the care a patient received had made them proud. The perspectives of physicians, nurses, janitors, and administrative staff were intertwined, and the focus was on positive real-life examples that captured Cleveland Clinic at its best.

The question posed was, What made the care great in this instance, and how could Cleveland Clinic make that greatness happen every time? The cost for taking its personnel offline for these exercises was estimated to be $11 million, but Cosgrove considers it one of the most powerful ways he helped the organization align around its mission.

Another tactic is to establish social norms that support the top-level goal. At Mayo Clinic the social norm for clinicians is to respond to pages about patients immediately. They don't finish driving to their destination; they pull off the road and call in. They don't finish writing an email or conclude a conversation, even with a patient. They excuse themselves and answer the page.

"What happens if you don't answer your beeper right away?" we asked several people at Mayo. "You won't do well here," several told us. Another joked, "The earth will open up and swallow you." A third said, "The last thing you want is to have people say, 'He's the kind of guy who doesn't answer his page.'" It's part of a bigger picture.

Gauging Your Grit

TO SEE HOW GRITTY YOU ARE COMPARED with a pool of more than 5,000 American adults, answer the questions below, tally your score, and divide by 10. Don't overthink your answers or try to guess the "right" answer. The more honestly you respond, the more accurate the results. (To take an online version of the test and get an instant score, go to angeladuckworth.com/grit-scale/.)

		Not at all like me ———→				Very much like me
1.	New ideas and projects sometimes distract me from previous ones.	5	4	3	2	1
2.	Setbacks don't discourage me. I don't give up easily.	1	2	3	4	5
3.	I often set a goal but later choose to pursue a different one.	5	4	3	2	1
4.	I am a hard worker.	1	2	3	4	5
5.	I have difficulty maintaining my focus on projects that take more than a few months to complete.	5	4	3	2	1
6.	I finish whatever I begin.	1	2	3	4	5
7.	My interests change from year to year.	5	4	3	2	1
8.	I am diligent. I never give up.	1	2	3	4	5
9.	I have been obsessed with a certain idea or project for a short time but later lost interest.	5	4	3	2	1
10.	I have overcome setbacks to conquer an important challenge.	1	2	3	4	5

Compare your results with the percentiles below to find out if you have more or less grit than average. If you scored at least 4.5, for instance, you are grittier than 90% of test takers.

Grit score	2.5	3.0	3.3	3.5	3.8	3.9	4.1	4.3	4.5	4.7	4.9
Percentile	10%	20%	30%	40%	50%	60%	70%	80%	90%	95%	99%

There is more to "the Mayo Way" than a dress code (and there is a dress code). It includes answering your beeper, working in teams, and putting patients' needs first.

Another fundamental characteristic of gritty organizations is restlessness with the status quo and an unrelenting drive to improve. Fostering that restlessness in a health care organization is a real test of leadership, because health care is full of people who are well trained and work hard—but often are not receptive to hearing that change is needed. However, a goal of "preserving our greatness" is not a compelling argument for change or an attraction for gritty employees. The focus instead should be on health care's true customers, patients—not just on providing pleasant "service" but on the endless quest to meet their medical and emotional needs.

It also helps to promote inside the organization something Stanford psychologist Carol Dweck calls a "growth mindset"—a belief that abilities can be developed through hard work and feedback, and that major challenges and setbacks provide an opportunity to learn. That, of course, requires leadership to accept, and even publicly communicate, complications and errors—something that doesn't always come easily in health care. But leaders that are explicit about the need for calculated risk taking, reducing mistakes, and continual learning tend to be the ones who actually inspire real growth in their organizations.

Crises offer special opportunities for growth—and in particular to strengthen culture. Organizations that have provided care after natural disasters or terrorist attacks have found that the experience leads to powerful bonding, a reinforced sense of purpose, the desire to excel, and a renewed commitment to organizational goals.

For example, when Hurricane Katrina hit New Orleans, in 2005, a local hospital affiliated with Ochsner Health System faced a series of incredible challenges, including power outages, flooding, overcrowding, and inadequate food and supplies. But throughout, morale remained high, because the employees all pulled together and performed duties outside their usual roles. Physicians served meals, for instance, and nurses cleaned units. "The team that was here throughout the storm has a relationship that can only be duplicated by soldiers in combat," the hospital's vice president of supply chain and support services told *Repertoire* magazine. "There's such respect and trust for one another."

Responding to self-generated crises can be a little trickier, however. But here, patient stories can be powerful drivers of improvement—especially if the stories are mortifying and involve "one of our own." At Henry Ford Health System, for example, every new employee watches a video depicting the experience of a physician in the system's intensive care unit, Rana Awdish, who nearly bled to death in the ICU in 2008 when a tumor in her liver suddenly ruptured. She was in severe shock and had a stroke; she was also seven months pregnant, and the baby did not survive.

As her conditioned worsened, Awdish heard her own colleagues say, "She's trying to die on us" and "She's circling the drain"—things that she herself had said when working in the same ICU. Hearing her describe her experience made her colleagues realize that her doctors were focused on the problem but not on her as a human being, and that this probably was happening a lot within Henry Ford. The crisis led leadership to commit to the goal of treating every patient with empathy all the time. Today every employee at Henry Ford has seen the video, and the goal of being reliably empathic is clearly understood. Sharing Awdish's story is just one of the interventions that has occurred at Henry Ford, and during the campaign that followed the organization saw most physician-related measures of patient experience improve by five to 10 percentage points.

The Gritty Leader

Ralph Waldo Emerson observed that organizations are the lengthened shadows of their leaders. To attract employees, build teams, and develop an organizational culture that all have grit, leaders should personify passion and perseverance—providing a visible, authoritative role model for every other person in the organization. And in their personal interactions, they too must be both demanding—keeping standards high—and supportive.

Consider Toby Cosgrove. He was a diligent student but, because he had dyslexia that was undiagnosed until his mid-thirties, his academic record was lackluster. Nevertheless, he set his sights on medical school, applying to 13. Just one, the University of Virginia, accepted him. In retrospect, "the dyslexia reinforced my determination and persistence," Cosgrove told us, "because I had to work more hours than anybody else to get the same result."

In 1968, Cosgrove's surgical residency was interrupted when he was drafted. He served a two-year tour as a U.S. Air Force surgeon in Vietnam. Upon his return home, he completed his residency and then joined Cleveland Clinic in 1975. "Everybody told me not to become a heart surgeon," he said. "I did it anyway." Indeed, Cosgrove performed more cardiac surgeries (about 22,000) than any of his contemporaries. He pioneered several technologies and innovations, including minimally invasive mitral valve surgery, earning more than 30 patents.

Cosgrove's development as a world-class surgeon is a case study in grit. "I was informed that I was the least talented individual in my residency. But failure is a great teacher. I worked and worked and worked at refining the craft," he told us. "I changed the way I did things over time. I used to take what I called 'innovation trips'—trips all over the world to watch other surgeons and their techniques. I'd pick things up from them and incorporate them in my practice. I was on a constant quest to find ways to do things better."

Cosgrove was named CEO of Cleveland Clinic in 2004. The passion and perseverance that made him great as a surgeon and as the head of a cardiac care team would soon be tested in his new role as leader of more than 43,000 employees. "I decided I had to become a student of leadership," Cosgrove recalls. "I had stacks of books on leadership, and every night when I came home, I would go up to my little office and read. And then I called up Harvard Business School professor Michael Porter." Porter, widely considered the father of the modern field of strategy, invited Cosgrove to visit. "He talked with me for two hours. After that, I got him to come to Cleveland. Since then, we've been sharing ideas," Cosgrove says. Porter helped him understand that as CEO he needed to be more than a renowned surgeon and an enthusiastic leader. He needed to evolve the organization's strategy, focusing on how to create value for patients and achieve competitive differentiation in the process.

Cosgrove scrutinized Cleveland Clinic's quality data, and while its mortality statistics were similar to those of other leading institutions, performance on other metrics—especially patient experience—left much to be desired. "People respected us," he says, "but they sure didn't like us." In 2009 he hired Jim Merlino, a young physician who had left the clinic unhappily after the death of his father there, and made him chief experience officer. Cosgrove asked Merlino to fix the things that had driven him away.

Cosgrove supported Merlino's many innovative ideas, including having all employees go through the appreciative inquiry exercise, and making an internal training film, an "empathy video" that is so powerful it has been watched by many outside the clinic, getting more than 4 million views on YouTube. As a result of these efforts and many others, Cleveland Clinic moved from the bottom quartile in patient experience to the top.

The institutional changes Cosgrove and his team have accomplished are too numerous to catalog, but here are a few: Swapping parking spaces so that patients, not doctors, are closest to the clinic's entrances. Moving medical records from hard copy to electronic storage. Developing standard care paths to ensure consistency and optimize the quality of care. Refusing to hire smokers and, recently, in response to the national opioid crisis, doing random drug testing of all Cleveland Clinic staff, including physicians and executives.

These changes weren't always popular when they were introduced. But when he knows he's right, Cosgrove stays the course. A placard he keeps on his desk reminds him "What can be conceived can be created."

It's hard to argue with the results achieved during his 13-year tenure as CEO. In addition to the improvements in patient experience, revenue grew from $3.7 billion in 2004 to $8.5 billion in 2016, and total annual visits increased from 2.8 million to 7.1 million. Quality on virtually every available metric has risen to the top tier of U.S. health care.

When Cosgrove gave his first big speech as CEO, he gave out 40,000 lapel buttons that said, "Patients First." We asked if some of his colleagues rolled their eyes. "Yes, a lot of them did," he said. "But I made the decision that I was going to pretend I didn't see them."

Cosgrove showed grit. And led an organization that has become his reflection.

Originally published in September–October 2018. **Reprint** R1805G

Leading in Times of Trauma

by Jane E. Dutton, Peter J. Frost, Monica C. Worline, Jacoba M. Lilius, and Jason M. Kanov

ONCE IN A GREAT WHILE, tragic circumstances present us with a challenge for which we simply cannot prepare. The terrorist attacks of last September immediately come to mind, but managers and their employees face crises at other times, too. Tragedies can occur at an individual level—an employee is diagnosed with cancer, for example, or loses a family member to an unexpected illness—or on a larger scale—a natural disaster destroys an entire section of a city, leaving hundreds of people dead, injured, or homeless. Such events can cause unspeakable pain not only for the people directly involved but also for those who see misfortune befall colleagues, friends, or even total strangers. That pain spills into the workplace.

The managerial rule books fail us at times like these, when people are searching for meaning and a reason to hope for the future. There is, however, something leaders can do in times of collective pain and confusion. By the very nature of your position, you can help individuals and companies begin to heal by taking actions that demonstrate your own compassion, thereby unleashing a compassionate response throughout the whole organization. Our research at the University of Michigan and the University of British Columbia's CompassionLab has demonstrated that although the human capacity to show compassion is universal, some organizations suppress it while others create an environment in which compassion is not only expressed but spreads.

Why is organizational compassion important, beyond the obvious and compelling reasons of humanity? Unleashing compassion in the workplace not only lessens the immediate suffering of those directly affected by trauma, it enables them to recover from future setbacks more quickly and effectively, and it increases their attachment to their colleagues and hence to the company itself. For those who witness or participate in acts of compassion, the effect is just as great; people's caring gestures contribute to their own resilience and attachment to the organization. Indeed, we've found that a leader's ability to enable a compassionate response throughout a company directly affects the organization's ability to maintain high performance in difficult times. It fosters a company's capacity to heal, to learn, to adapt, and to excel.

In the following pages, we will describe the actions leaders can take to enable organizational compassion in times of trauma. Before we begin, it's worth noting that some of our examples draw from the events of September 11, 2001, because the magnitude of pain surrounding those events was unprecedented in business history and because the public nature of those events makes the stories relevant to a broad audience. However, pain occurred in the workplace long before last September, and individual and group traumas will continue to disrupt people's daily routines—at times, shattering their lives—as long as humans continue to conduct business.

Beyond Empathy

When people think of compassion, the first thing that comes to mind for many is empathy. But while empathy can be comforting, it does not engender a broader response and therefore has limited capacity for organizational healing. Instead, our research shows that compassionate leadership involves taking some form of public action, however small, that is intended to ease people's pain—and that inspires others to act as well.

TJX president and CEO Edmond English, who lost seven employees aboard one of the planes that hit the World Trade Center, gathered his staff together shortly after the attacks to confirm the names

Idea in Brief

The unspeakable happens: A beloved leader dies; a fire leaves dozens homeless; terrorists kill thousands.

Traumatic events cause incalculable pain for victims and all who care about them—pain that spills into the workplace and overwhelms employees. As a leader, you can't eliminate the suffering. But you *can* ease the collective anguish and confusion.

How? By demonstrating your own compassion and unleashing a companywide **compassionate response**. When you help people make sense of terrible events and support one another, you enhance their capacity to heal and strengthen bonds among colleagues and with the organization. Bolstered by these bonds, your company can adapt, even excel, during difficult times.

of the victims. He called in grief counselors the very same day and chartered a plane to bring the victims' relatives from Canada and Europe to the company's headquarters in Framingham, Massachusetts. He personally greeted the families when they arrived in the parking lot at midnight on September 15. Although told by English that they could take some time off after the attacks, most employees opted to come in to work, as English himself had done, and support one another in the early days following the tragedy.

For a historical perspective on the same kind of compassionate leadership, we can look to Britain's Queen Mother, who demonstrated great courage by refusing to leave London as bombs ravaged the city around her during World War II. She and King George visited sites that had been destroyed during the Blitz of 1940, showing her dedication, concern, and commitment to the Allied cause, and inspiring lifelong admiration and loyalty for her constant presence.

In vivid contrast, immediately following the terrorist attacks in New York City, leaders at a publishing company close to ground zero refused to disrupt business as usual. The company held regularly scheduled meetings the day after the attacks and provided little or no support for people to share and express their pain. One editor told us she'd gotten a call at home early on the morning of September 12,

Idea in Practice

Find Meaning amid Chaos

Create an environment where people can freely express emotions and explore questions such as "Why did this happen? How will we cope?" No longer forced to suppress their feelings *at* work, they can refocus *on* work—which itself can be healing.

- **Openly express your own feelings.** Mayor Rudolph Giuliani's public display of grief after the September 11th New York terrorist attacks enabled a city-wide expression of anguish—and strengthened people's resolve.

- **Be present—physically and emotionally.** The CEO of a research firm that lost a senior executive to a heart attack delivered the news to each management team member individually—at their homes. As he quietly sat with them, he embodied the company's caring and helped them begin processing the tragedy.

- **Communicate company values**—to remind people about their work's larger purpose as they grapple with a trauma.

Example:

When *Newsweek's* editor Maynard Parker fell terminally ill, the editor-in-chief immediately re-emphasized the company's—and Parker's—commitment to community and world-class reporting. Employees honored Parker's values by doing their best work, while sharing their sorrow over his leukemia. *Newsweek* then emerged as a leader in coverage of a major news event.

just as she was trying to help her eight-year-old daughter make sense of what had happened the day before, demanding to know why she was late for a meeting. She went to work and sat through a four-hour conference call but was present in body only. Because she was given no opportunity to connect with her family, friends, and colleagues and was offered little organizational comfort in the face of a terrifying and confusing sequence of events, she felt her loyalty to the company eroding with every passing minute.

What English and other leaders have done—and what the leaders of the publishing company failed to do—is facilitate a compassionate institutional response on two levels. The first level is what we call

Inspire Action amid Agony

Create an environment where people can alleviate their own and others' suffering. You'll unleash companywide compassion and healing.

- **Model behaviors you'd like others to demonstrate.** When a fire destroyed the University of Michigan's student housing, the dean interrupted an important speech with reassuring remarks—and wrote a personal check. His actions catalyzed campus-wide relief efforts.

- **Use your influence to reallocate needed resources.** When a hospital employee's husband suffered kidney failure and was awaiting a transplant, the billing-department manager gave her a pager and organized a team to shoulder her work at a moment's notice.

- **Use existing systems to mobilize resources.** After two Macy's stores suffered severe earthquake damage, managers used the payroll system to deliver cash to employees who had lost homes and needed shelter, and the human resources system to place them in other stores.

- **Support bottom-up compassion.** In organizations that inspire compassion, initiatives bubble from the bottom *and* top. When a Michigan hospital's employees donated $18,000+ worth of their vacation time to the Red Cross after the September terrorist attacks, the company matched the amount.

a *context for meaning*—the leader creates an environment in which people can freely express and discuss the way they feel, which in turn helps them to make sense of their pain, seek or provide comfort, and imagine a more hopeful future. The second level is a *context for action*—the leader creates an environment in which those who experience or witness pain can find ways to alleviate their own and others' suffering. We have undertaken in-depth studies of leaders at organizations facing all manner of crises, and we have found that those who excel at leading compassionately and effectively in times of crisis adhere to a set of shared practices that help people make sense of terrible events and allow employees to move on.

Meaning amid Chaos

Acute trauma, tragedy, or distress can cause people to engage in intense soul-searching. We aren't referring to the restlessness and stocktaking that are a natural and ongoing process as people mature and grow in their careers; we're talking about the persistent and vexing questions that affect how people live their lives: Why did this happen? Could I have prevented it? How will we cope? Why me? And even, for employees who witness a tragic event but are not directly affected, why *not* me?

It isn't your job as a leader to answer these questions. But at the same time, it's not realistic or reasonable to ask people to ponder these questions only on their own time, outside the office. Instead, you can cultivate an environment that allows people to work through these questions in their own way so they can eventually start assigning meaning to events and begin healing.

You can start by setting an example for others by openly revealing your own humanity. You may well experience the same emotions affecting your employees—from deep sorrow to anxiousness to uncertainty to anger to steely resolve. Openly expressing these feelings can be very powerful for those who witness it, especially during times of extreme pain. Mayor Rudolph Giuliani's public display of grief in the wake of the New York terrorist attacks set the stage for an honest expression of anguish throughout the city and, at the same time, strengthened people's resolve to rebuild and restore confidence in the city. When people know they can bring their pain to the office, they no longer have to expend energy trying to ignore or suppress it, and they can more easily and effectively get back to work. This may be a mutually reinforcing cycle, since getting back to a routine can be healing in itself.

Conversely, when you expect people to stifle their emotions, they don't know how and where to direct their energies, and it's very difficult for them to figure out how to focus at work. It can also test their loyalty to the organization. We interviewed employees at an architectural firm where a visitor died suddenly in the firm's hallways despite employees' heroic efforts to revive him. Company leaders did not acknowledge the trauma publicly, leaving people shocked and demoralized—and uncertain about how to respond should such an event occur again. Some employees were wracked with guilt over not being able to save the man's life. Others felt weak and helpless because they had no opportunity to grieve in the presence of their colleagues. They had shared a significant experience and could not console one another—or even recognize people's extraordinary efforts to revive the victim. This one event damaged not just the employees who were directly involved but also the social fabric of the whole company. By acting as if nothing out of the ordinary had happened, the company's leaders left people feeling as if the organization didn't recognize them as human beings, which created a rift between employees and management that has never been repaired.

A seemingly simple but important aspect of demonstrating your humanity is just being present, physically and emotionally. It shows employees that the organization cares about what happens to them and will do whatever it can to help them in a time of need. At one leading market-research firm, a senior executive died suddenly of a heart attack. The grief-stricken CEO personally visited each member of his 20-person management team to deliver the news, going house to house to share in each person's sorrow. His presence couldn't undo their colleague's death, nor could it stop their pain. But there is tremendous power in just sitting with people as they process terrible events. Bear in mind, too, that being there doesn't mean you have to visit people at home. Sitting with someone who's going through a crisis in his or her office can be just as powerful.

It isn't necessarily words that matter at times like these. Indeed, the dean of a divinity school told us that when a close relative died unexpectedly, he had been most comforted by one couple who arrived at his house and simply wept with him. To this day he remembers their very presence as a powerful moment of healing. Unfortunately, however, the simple act of being there doesn't come easily or naturally to most people. It can be much easier to avoid those who are in pain. One CEO in our research told us that his natural tendency had been to shrink from addressing people's personal

Measuring Organizational Compassion

FOR A QUICK, HIGH-LEVEL CHECK on your organization's capacity for compassion, consider how it performs on the following four dimensions. Each indicator is a measure of the organization's compassion competence, which helps people to heal and continue on with their work when times are bad:

The **scope** of compassionate response refers to the breadth of resources provided to people in need, such as money, work flexibility, physical aid, and other people's time and attention. If an employee falls ill, is time off the only support, or does the system supply a wide range of healing resources such as variable work hours, gestures of comfort (like food, flowers, and cards), financial support, and assistance with child care?

The **scale** of compassionate response gauges the volume of resources, time, and attention that people who are suffering receive. Companies that are most effective at unleashing organizational compassion match the scale to the need. When a block of apartments was destroyed in a fire, the people who lived in the apartments, who worked for different companies, found a wide variation in how their companies responded. Some received a routine distribution of insurance coverage. Others were astonished at the outpouring of help from both corporate channels and individual colleagues—money, housewares, furniture, and offers of places to stay. In the latter case, the compassion competence of the system is more likely to help employees heal

---

problems—until the sudden death of his own son revealed for him the power of other people's presence.

Leaders can also help people in times of trauma by taking care of their basic needs, which gives people room to make meaning of events for themselves and allows them to focus on coping with the crisis. This is one reason people bring food to friends who have suffered a death in the family, but it can apply to organizations as well. At one consulting firm we studied, an employee's daughter suffered an horrific car accident far from home. To make it easier for the employee and her husband, the company's leaders rented an apartment for them near the hospital. Knowing that they had a safe and close place to stay removed one aspect of the family's stress and allowed them to focus on their daughter's health.

In another example, the wife of a terminally ill employee at Cisco Systems was so taxed with caring for her husband that she

faster even as it strengthens their loyalty to the company—among those who experienced the tragedy directly and among those who witnessed and participated in the response.

Speed of response can vary widely as well. Companies with a competence for compassion extract and direct resources quickly, with little hesitation. Responding compassionately is a hardwired capability. Even in highly regimented bureaucracies, compassion can kick in quickly. In one manufacturing organization, a manager suffered a severe head injury that required almost three months of recovery. This was just after he had been appointed to lead an important experimental project that removed him from the regular compensation scheme and placed him on an incentive pay and benefits system. His previous job had been filled, and he was effectively stuck in no-man's land. A senior operations manager swiftly reinstated the man's previous compensation, obtaining the necessary sign-off without delay, an act that allayed the family's anxiety over its financial circumstances.

Specialization measures the degree to which the system customizes resources to the particular needs of an individual or a group in pain. If, for example, several employees' children are injured in a bus accident, some families will need close communication and hands-on comforting. Others will need to grieve privately and get back to work quickly.

couldn't find the time to make him a pot roast, his favorite dinner, on his birthday. Barbara Beck, a senior vice president at the company, decided she would cook a pot roast and deliver it to the family herself. The gesture lent a semblance of normalcy to the occasion and gave the employee's wife the space she needed to cope with her husband's illness and to process its effects on her life. In yet another case, the branch manager at a bank, whose close friend and second-in-command died of a heart attack, took on numerous extra duties and clients so his employees would have additional time to mourn—even as he himself was suffering tremendous grief.

This meaning-making process can also be supported by communicating and reinforcing organizational values—reminding people about the larger purpose of their work even as they struggle to make sense of major life issues. When *Newsweek* employees were coping with the unexpected illness and death of editor Maynard Parker, the magazine's editor-in-chief, Richard Smith, at once emphasized the company's commitment to community and its commitment to remaining a world-class newsmagazine. He created an environment in which people could do their best work and at the same time share their sorrow over Parker's losing battle with leukemia. Smith gave daily updates on Parker's condition and stressed that the company was actively involved in getting him top medical care. Knowing that they had ample opportunities to talk about their feelings, and that Parker was getting the best care possible, the *Newsweek* staff could then concentrate on honoring the publication's commitment to remaining a leading newsmagazine—which was particularly meaningful because Parker had so enthusiastically pursued this goal himself. The year's most significant news event was breaking just as Parker fell ill, and *Newsweek* emerged as a leader in the coverage in part because employees wanted to honor Parker in the way he would have valued most-by showing tremendous loyalty in an industry marked by high turnover.

Mark Whitaker, who was then managing editor and succeeded Parker as editor, has reflected on how Smith and others at the top of the organization provided meaning for people that could sustain them through the crisis and beyond. "I think it made people realize, 'Well, if I ever have a situation like that myself, God forbid, this is a company that will be there for me.' That is an intangible thing, but I think it's very powerful," Whitaker recalls. "The way that you deal with tragedy and illness and misfortune in the lives not only of your top people but of all your people really defines your values as an organization."

The Benjamin Group, a Silicon Valley–based public relations firm, demonstrates its values by taking a stand on how employees are treated not only by their colleagues and managers but also by their customers, suppliers, and other business partners. CEO Sheri Benjamin has established a code of principles that includes the statement "We're all in this together," and one implication is that if a client is consistently abusive to firm members, the firm will resign the account. A few years ago, the company dropped a million-dollar account—at that time, worth fully 20% of its annual business. Employees were startled that the firm would go so far, but they were energized, too: Inspired by the knowledge that the PR firm cared about their wellbeing, they worked extra hard to bring in new clients.

A final note on meaning-making: Symbolic gestures can be very powerful. Two days after the September 11 terrorist attacks, England's Queen Elizabeth II asked her troops to play *The Star-Spangled Banner* during the changing of the guard services outside Buckingham Palace. This extraordinary break from a time-honored tradition, dating back to 1660, gave thousands of Americans far from home, as well as supporters from other countries, a way to pay their respects and to mourn.

Actions amid Agony

A context for meaning is the all-important backdrop for creating a compassionate organization, but it is in creating a context for action that leaders can truly unleash an organization's power to heal. As a leader you can set the right example to awaken the potential for compassion, and you can prompt the organizational infrastructure to reinforce and institutionalize compassionate acts.

Perhaps the most important step you can take is to model the behaviors you would like to see others demonstrate. Frequently, people aren't sure if it's appropriate to bring personal matters into the workplace, or they may simply not know how. You can show them, using your status and visibility as a leader.

When a fire destroyed some student living quarters at the University of Michigan Business School, former dean B. Joseph White interrupted his annual "state of the school" speech—typically heavily scripted and highly formal—with some strikingly personal remarks. He assured displaced students that the school would house them and wrote a personal check on the spot to pledge his support. Word of White's actions spread fast, catalyzing a campuswide effort to tap alumni, faculty, and staff networks to find housing, financial support, and other resources for the students affected by the fire.

Leaders can also use their influence to reallocate resources to support people in need. We spoke with the manager of a billing department at one hospital who makes it a point to know the work-loads and the personal circumstances of each member of her unit; that way, she can cut people slack when they need extra support. For example, when one employee's husband suffered kidney failure and was awaiting a transplant, the billing manager gave the woman a pager and organized a team of people who could step in and pick up the woman's work on a moment's notice. That way, the employee would be able to take her husband to the hospital without delay if a kidney became available.

In the wake of the September 11 attacks, the MWW Group, a pub-lic relations firm based in East Rutherford, New Jersey, juggled its resources so that people could take time off to volunteer at relief organizations. We've also seen leaders redirect funds intended for other purposes to pay for grief counselors in times of collective trauma.

When tragedy strikes, a company's existing infrastructure (its formal and informal networks and routines) can be helpful in locat-ing useful resources, generating ideas, coordinating groups that are not typically connected, and communicating to people what is happening and how the company is responding. For example, after two Macy's stores were badly damaged in the 1994 Northridge, Cali-fornia, earthquake and could not immediately reopen, a store man-ager used the payroll system to quickly deliver cash to employees whose homes were destroyed. Macy's issued emergency advances of up to $1,000 at a time so that people could secure food, water, and shelter for their families. Following the immediate relief effort, the human resources team used its standard placement routines to search among Macy's stores in Southern California for oppor-tunities to put displaced workers back on the job right away. HR workers quickly determined where help was most needed and then used their networks of employees to establish car pools for people. Within a short time, all employees and undamaged stores were up and running again. People often think of routines as unwieldy pro-cesses that interfere with quick response. But in Macy's case, as at other companies we've studied, the established routines helped to expedite matters.

Companies can also set up new routines or networks designed specifically to accelerate aid in the event of a crisis. After a Cisco employee developed a medical emergency while visiting Japan and couldn't find an English-speaking health care provider, the company wanted to make sure that no other employee would ever feel so alone in such a frightening circumstance. So it designed a network that would furnish medical assistance to any member of the Cisco family traveling abroad. Interestingly, that network has proved valuable in unexpected ways. In 1998, for instance, civil strife in Indonesia put Jakarta-based employees in the midst of conflict. The company Cisco used to provide international health services sent an ambulance to Cisco's Jakarta headquarters—an ambulance could travel through the streets where no ordinary car could. Employees were loaded into the ambulance, hidden beneath blankets, and driven to a deserted army airstrip where a waiting aircraft took them to safety.

From the Bottom Up

It's essential to note that organizational response doesn't have to start at the top. Leaders need to recognize and support instances where spontaneous organizing and compassionate actions occur at the lower levels of a company. When the organizational context emphasizes and inspires compassionate responses, bottom-up initiatives can take hold and have a transformative effect. Indeed, much of the assistance following the fire at the University of Michigan was generated by staff and students. One student, who did not even know the victims very well, organized more than 40 other students to recreate all the classroom notes from two years of MBA studies and delivered the study materials to the victims within a week of the fire.

At Foote Hospital in Jackson, Michigan, employees wanted to help a colleague who had lost three close relatives, so they lobbied for a system that would let them donate vacation or personal time to others who needed extra days off. Donating time has now become an official policy at Foote—although, of course, contributions are voluntary—thanks to the initiative and innovative thinking of people at the staff level of the organization. This program took on new life in the wake of the attacks in New York and Washington, DC. Foote employees donated more than $18,000 worth of their vacation time to the Red Cross relief fund—again, at their own initiative—and the hospital matched this amount.

At *Newsweek,* one employee organized a blood and platelet donation drive when Maynard Parker fell ill, another managed home chores for Parker's family, and yet another babysat his children. Another bottom-up response arose when Morgan Stanley was devastated by the World Trade Center attacks and had no immediate way to keep track of who was affected. Customer-service representatives from another division of the company took the initiative to organize a vital service: They collected employee information and created a Web site to help the company respond to the needs of individual families.

As these stories show, organizational compassion can be contagious. Indeed, what we call "positive spirals of compassion," where one act of compassion inspires another, are common. At the University of Michigan, for example, MBA students organized a fundraiser to support victims of the huge earthquake in India last May. When they heard about the relief effort, the leaders of several student clubs contributed the remainder of their club budgets to the drive.

The Case for Compassion

It's hard to document the positive effect that organizational compassion has on employee retention and productivity, but it's clear that employees will reward companies that treat them humanely. On December 11, 1995, a fire destroyed the Malden Mills manufacturing plant in Massachusetts. Instead of taking his $300 million insurance payout and relocating or retiring, owner Aaron Feuerstein decided to rebuild the factory. He announced that he would keep all 3,000 employees on the payroll through December while he started to rebuild. In January, he said he would pay them for a second month, and in February, Feuerstein pledged to pay for a third. His generosity made quite an impact on his employees: Productivity at the plant nearly doubled once it reopened.

Conversely, the costs of not providing leadership and the organizational infrastructure to help people deal with their grief are considerable. People in pain tend to be distracted at work, and if they don't have appropriate outlets, they may become unresponsive and even uncooperative in dealing with colleagues and customers. Just as compassion can be contagious, so can the detachment that accompanies a noncompassionate response; loyalty to the organization erodes not just among people who have directly suffered a tragedy but also among their colleagues who witness the lack of care. Over time, if an organization will not or cannot support the healing process, employee retention will suffer.

At one newspaper, a newsroom manager lost his wife to breast cancer. During his wife's extended illness, the employee felt no compassion from his boss; instead he endured complaints about his relatively low level of production. On his first day back to work after the funeral his boss said, "I guess you'll be working those 12-hour days again." The journalist, who was now raising two young children on his own, quit. In another example, a health care employee finally got pregnant after many years of trying, only to deliver a stillborn baby in her eighth month. When the woman's boss stopped by her hospital room, she assumed he was there to offer his condolences. Instead he had come to ask her when she would return to work. Shocked at his lack of compassion, the woman applied to be transferred to another unit, and her manager—who ran a very busy and stretched unit—lost a valued employee with more than 10 years of experience.

As a colleague of ours once remarked, there is always grief somewhere in the room. One person may be feeling personal pain due to a death in the family. Another may find personality conflicts in the workplace unbearable. Still another may be watching a colleague struggle with a serious illness and not know how to help. You can't eliminate such suffering, nor can you ask people to check their emotions at the door. But you can use your leadership to begin the healing process. Through your presence you can model behaviors that set the stage for the process of making meaning out of terrible events. And through your actions you can empower people to find their own ways to support one another during painful times. This is a kind of leadership we wish we would never have to use, yet it is vital if we are to nourish the very humanity that can make people— and organizations—great.

Originally published in January 2002. Reprint 8563

Learning from the Future

by J. Peter Scoblic

HOW CAN WE FORMULATE strategy in the face of uncertainty?

That's the fundamental question leaders must ask as they prepare for the future. And in the midst of a global pandemic, answering it has never felt more urgent.

Even before the Covid-19 crisis, rapid technological change, growing economic interdependence, and mounting political instability had conspired to make the future increasingly murky. Uncertainty was so all-encompassing that to fully capture the dimensions of the problem, researchers had devised elaborate acronyms such as VUCA (volatility, uncertainty, complexity, and ambiguity) and TUNA (turbulent, uncertain, novel, and ambiguous).

In response, many leaders sought refuge in the more predictable short term—a mechanism for coping with uncertainty that research has shown leaves billions of dollars of earnings on the table and millions of people needlessly unemployed. By the start of 2020, the sense of uncertainty was so pervasive that many executives were doubling down on efficiency at the expense of innovation, favoring the present at the expense of the future.

And then the pandemic hit.

Now the tyranny of the present is supreme. A lot of organizations have had no choice but to focus on surviving immediate threats. (There are no futurists in foxholes.) But many business and political discussions still demand farsightedness. The stakes are high, and decisions that leaders make now may have ramifications for years—or even decades. As they try to manage their way through the crisis, they need a way to link current moves to future outcomes.

So how best to proceed?

Strategic foresight—the history, theory, and practice of which I have spent years researching—offers a way forward. Its aim is not to predict the future but rather to make it possible to imagine multiple futures in creative ways that heighten our ability to sense, shape, and adapt to what happens in the years ahead. Strategic foresight doesn't help us figure out *what* to think about the future. It helps us figure out *how* to think about it.

To be sure, a growing body of research has demonstrated that it is possible to make more-accurate predictions, even in chaotic fields like geopolitics. We should use those techniques to the extent we can. But when predictive tools reach their limits, we need to turn to strategic foresight, which takes the irreducible uncertainty of the future as a starting point. In that distinctive context, it helps leaders make better decisions.

The most recognizable tool of strategic foresight is scenario planning. It involves several stages: identifying forces that will shape future market and operating conditions; exploring how those drivers may interact; imagining a variety of plausible futures; revising mental models of the present on the basis of those futures; and then using those new models to devise strategies that prepare organizations for whatever the future actually brings.

Today the use of scenarios is widespread. But all too often, organizations conduct just a single exercise and then set whatever they learn from it on the shelf. If companies want to make effective strategy in the face of uncertainty, they need to set up a process of constant exploration—one that allows top managers to build permanent but flexible bridges between their actions in the present and their thinking about the future. What's necessary, in short, is not just imagination but the *institutionalization* of imagination. That is the essence of strategic foresight.

Idea in Brief

The Challenge

Good strategy creates competitive advantage over time, but the uncertainty of the future makes it difficult to identify effective courses of action, particularly in the midst of a crisis. As a leader, how can you prepare for an unpredictable future while managing the urgent demands of the present?

The Promise

The practice of strategic foresight provides the capacity to sense, shape, and adapt to change as it happens. One important element of the practice is scenario planning, which helps leaders navigate uncertainty by teaching them how to anticipate possible futures while still operating in the present.

The Way Forward

To make effective strategy in the face of uncertainty, leaders need to institutionalize strategic foresight, harnessing the power of imagination to build a dynamic link between planning and operations.

The Limits of Experience

Uncertainty stems from our inability to compare the present to anything we've previously experienced. When situations lack analogies to the past, we have trouble envisioning how they will play out in the future.

The economist Frank Knight famously argued that uncertainty is best understood in contrast with risk. In situations of risk, Knight wrote, we can calculate the probability of particular outcomes, because we have seen many similar situations before. (A life insurance company, for example, has data on enough 45-year-old, non-smoking white men to estimate how long one of them is going to live.) But in situations of uncertainty—and Knight put most business decisions in this category—we can only guess what might happen, because we lack the experience to gauge the most likely outcome. In fact, we might not even be able to imagine the range of potential outcomes.

The key in those situations, Knight felt, was judgment. Managers with good judgment can successfully chart a course through uncertainty despite a lack of reference points. Unfortunately, Knight had no idea where good judgment came from. He called it an "unfathomable mystery."

Of course, in something of a catch-22, conventional wisdom holds that to a large extent good judgment is based on experience. And in many uncertain situations managers do, in fact, turn to historical analogy to anticipate the future. This is why business schools use the case teaching method: It's a way of exposing students to a range of analogies—and thus ostensibly helping them develop judgment— much more quickly than is possible in the normal course of life.

But Knight's point was that uncertainty is marked by novelty, which, by definition, lacks antecedents. At the very moment when the present least resembles the past, it makes little sense to look back in time for clues about the future. In times of uncertainty, we run up against the limits of experience, so we must look elsewhere for judgment.

That's where strategic foresight comes in.

"Strange Aids to Thought"

In the United States, strategic foresight can be traced back to the RAND Corporation, a think tank that the U.S. Air Force set up after World War II. Rather than plumbing the mystery of judgment, RAND scholars hoped to replace it with the "rational" tools of quantitative analysis. But as they grappled with the military demands of the postwar world, they could not escape the fact that nuclear weapons had fundamentally changed the nature of warfare. Two countries, the United States and the Soviet Union, had acquired the ability to destroy each other as functioning civilizations. And because no one had ever fought a nuclear war before, no one knew how best to fight (or avoid) one.

One RAND analyst, who approached the problem of a potential apocalypse with a glee that made him a model for Stanley Kubrick's Dr. Strangelove, was a mathematician named Herman Kahn. In the atomic age, Kahn realized, military strategists faced uncertainty to an absolutely unprecedented degree. "Nuclear war is still (and hopefully will remain) so far from our experience," he wrote, "that it is difficult to reason from, or illustrate arguments by, analogies from history."

How, then, Kahn asked, could military strategists develop the judgment crucial to making decisions about an uncertain future? It was the very question Knight had posed, but unlike Knight, Kahn had an answer: "ersatz experience." What strategists needed, he suggested, were "strange aids to thought," in the form of multiple imagined futures that could be developed through simulations such as war games and scenarios.

In 1961, Kahn left RAND to help found the Hudson Institute, where he eventually shared his ideas with Pierre Wack, an executive from Royal Dutch Shell. In the early 1970s Wack famously applied Kahn's ideas in the business world, by devising scenarios to help Shell prepare for what might take place as the oil-rich nations of the Middle East began to assert themselves on the world stage. When change did come, in the form of the price shocks induced by the 1973 OPEC oil embargo, Shell was able to ride the crisis out much better than its competitors. (In 1985, Wack chronicled Shell's efforts in two articles for this magazine: "Scenarios: Uncharted Waters Ahead" and "Scenarios: Shooting the Rapids.")

The Shell exercises marked the birth of scenario planning as a strategic tool for business managers. In subsequent years, Wack's successors at the company refined his method, and scenario planners from Shell went on to become some of the most prominent scholars and practitioners in the field. Nonetheless, few of the organizations that have conducted scenario-planning exercises in recent decades have institutionalized them as part of a broader effort to achieve strategic foresight.

One of the rare exceptions is the U.S. Coast Guard, which describes its work with scenario planning as part of a "cycle of strategic renewal." As such, it offers a model that many organizations can learn from.

One might ask how relevant the Coast Guard's experience is for businesses, but in fact it constitutes what social scientists call a "crucial-case test." As a military service, the Coast Guard has less organizational flexibility than most private firms, with a mission mandated by statute and a budget determined by Congress. What's more, for a long time its need to react daily to numerous emerging situations—from ships in distress to drug interdictions—forced it to focus almost exclusively on the short term, leaving it with little bandwidth to formulate strategy for the long term. Nevertheless, in recent years it has managed to leverage scenario planning to its advantage, reorienting the organization in an ongoing way toward the future. And that, in turn, has allowed it to respond and adapt to disruptive changes, such as those that followed the September 11 terrorist attacks.

Future-Proofing the Coast Guard

On that tragic morning, hundreds of thousands of people found themselves trapped in Lower Manhattan, desperate to escape the burning chaos that was Ground Zero. While some were able to walk uptown or across bridges, which officials had closed to vehicles, for many the best way off the island was by water. So over the next hours, an impromptu flotilla—of ferries, tugs, private craft, and fire and police boats—took clusters of people away from the wreckage of the World Trade Center and across the water to safety.

Although many vessels operated on their own initiative, a significant part of the evacuation was directed by the Coast Guard, which had issued a call for "all available boats" and coordinated the chaotic debarkation with remarkable poise, creativity, and efficiency. The effort reminded many of the storied British evacuation across the English Channel of several hundred thousand troops that Nazi forces had trapped in Dunkirk, on the coast of France.

That the Coast Guard rose to the challenge is no surprise. Although it has a broad set of responsibilities, ranging from search-and-rescue to environmental protection to port security, the organization's motto is *Semper paratus*, or "Always ready," and it prides itself on responding to emergencies. As one retired captain told me, "Our whole idea is, when the alarm goes off, to be able to fly into action."

But September 11 ended up being more than a short-term challenge. In its aftermath, the Coast Guard found its mission quickly expanding. Within a day it was tasked with implementing radically heightened port-security measures around the country: Port security had previously accounted for 1% to 2% of its daily operational load, but it soon consumed 50% to 60%. In March 2003 the Coast Guard was integrated into the new Department of Homeland Security, and that same month it was given the job of securing ports and waterways all over Iraq, following the U.S.-led invasion. In subsequent years the service's budget would double and its ranks would swell. A new future had arrived.

The Coast Guard adapted to this future nimbly—and did so in part because in the late 1990s it had conducted a scenario-planning exercise called Project Long View, which was designed to help the organization contend with "a startlingly complex future operating environment characterized by new or unfamiliar security threats." Its aim, in effect, was to future-proof the Coast Guard.

The service ran Long View in 1998 and 1999—and then, in 2003, in response to the shocks of September 11, renamed it Project Evergreen and began running it every four years. Ever since, the organization has relied on Evergreen to help its leaders think and act strategically.

Robust Strategy—No Matter What the Future Holds

When the Coast Guard decided to launch Long View, it enlisted the help of the Futures Strategy Group (FSG), a consultancy specializing in scenario planning. FSG maintains that uncertainty precludes prediction but demands anticipation—and that imaginatively and rigorously exploring plausible futures can facilitate decision-making.

Working with FSG, the Coast Guard identified four forces for change that would have a significant impact on its future: the role of the federal government, the strength of the U.S. economy, the seriousness of threats to U.S. society, and the demand for maritime services. By exploring them and looking forward some 20 years, the team came up with 16 possible "far-future worlds" in which the Coast Guard might have to operate. Of those, Coast Guard leaders selected five that were as distinct as possible from one another (while remaining plausible) and represented the range of environments the

The Future: A Glossary

MANAGING THE UNCERTAINTY of the future requires many tools, some of which have similar or even overlapping functions. To cut through the confusion, here's a brief guide.

Backcasting asks participants to work backward in time from a particular future to ascertain what in the present caused its emergence. The practice is most often used to identify a path to a preferred future but can also be used to avoid steps toward a negative future. "Premortems," for example, aim to identify the causes of a hypothetical future failure.

Contingency planning aids decision-making by preparing participants for specific events that are considered possible or even likely. A contingency plan provides a playbook in case of emergency.

Crisis simulations and tabletop exercises have participants respond to specific scenarios and then analyze their actions, to help people prepare for real-life situations. They differ from war games in that they involve a specific possible future rather than a range of plausible futures.

Forecasting involves making probabilistic predictions about the future and, as such, is a tool that practitioners of strategic foresight tend to avoid. But it, too, has its place in helping strategists manage uncertainty, adding a quantitative angle to the qualitative methods preferred by, say, scenario planners. The best approach is this: Predict what you can; imagine what you cannot; and develop the judgment to know the difference.

Horizon scanning asks participants to search for "weak signals" of change in the present with an eye toward monitoring their development and assessing their potential impact. The practice is guided by the idea that the future often first comes into view in places that most of us are not paying attention to, such as specialized scientific journals.

Scenario planning uses stories about alternative futures to challenge assumptions and reframe perceptions of the present. The process does not attempt to predict the future but instead aims to explore plausible futures to inform strategy.

Trend analysis asks participants to consider the potential influence of patterns of change that are already visible. A popular structured approach is the STEEP framework, which disaggregates patterns of change into five categories: social, teohnologioal, economic, environmental, and political.

War games ask participants to engage an opponent in simulated conflict, often to explore reactions to novel circumstances. Like scenario planning, war games do not attempt to predict what will happen; rather, they project what could happen, thereby providing insight into decision-making. Despite the name, war games can address far more than just the military aspects of conflict.

service might face. FSG then wrote detailed descriptions of those futures and the fictional events that led to them.

Each future world was given a name intended to capture its essence. "Taking on Water" described a future in which the U.S. economy struggled amid significant environmental degradation. In "Pax Americana," a humbled United States had to contend with a world rent by political instability and economic catastrophe. "Planet Enterprise" was dominated by giant transnational corporations. "Pan-American Highway" featured regional trade blocs oriented around the dollar and the euro. And "Balkanized America" presciently warned of a divided world in which "terrorism strikes with frightening frequency, and increasingly close to home."

Using those scenarios, the Coast Guard convened a three-day workshop, which FSG facilitated. Teams of civilians and officers were assigned to different future worlds and charged with devising strategies that would enable the Coast Guard to operate effectively in them. At the end of the workshop the teams compared notes on what they had come up with. Strategies that appeared again and again, across different teams, were deemed "robust." In their final report the organizers of Long View listed 10 of these strategies, ranging from the creation of a more unified command structure to the development of a more flexible human-resources system to the establishment of "full maritime domain awareness"—which the Coast Guard defines as the "ability to acquire, track, and identify in real time any vessel or aircraft entering America's maritime domain." All of these strategies, they argued, would help the Coast Guard carry out its mission, no matter what the future held.

Many of the strategies weren't novel. But Long View allowed participants to think about them in new ways that proved crucial in the post–September 11 world. In effect, Long View allowed the Coast Guard to pressure-test strategies under a range of plausible futures, prioritize the most-promising ones, and socialize them among the leadership—which meant that after the attacks, when the organization found its mission changing dramatically, it was able to respond quickly.

Launching Long View and subsequently establishing Evergreen as a continuous process wasn't easy. It took exceptionally strong leadership—in particular from admirals James Loy and Thad Allen. The program has also faced challenges in implementing ideas; there is a difference between strategic foresight and strategic execution. But once established, the program developed significant momentum, fueled in part by a growing cadre of alumni who saw the value of a dynamic relationship between the present and the future. The Coast Guard had institutionalized imagination.

Exploration Enables Exploitation

Long View and Evergreen weren't designed to bring about a wholesale organizational shift from the operational to the strategic or to train the Coast Guard's attention primarily on the long term. Instead, the goal was to get its personnel thinking about the future in a way that would inform and improve their ability to operate in the present.

That was no small challenge. Management scholars have long noted that, in order to survive and thrive over time, organizations need to both exploit existing competencies and explore new ones. They need to be "ambidextrous."

The problem is that those two imperatives compete for resources, demand distinct ways of thinking, and require different organizational structures. Doing one makes it harder to do the other. Ambidexterity requires managers to somehow resolve this paradox.

Long View and Evergreen helped the service's leaders do that. The programs didn't reduce the organization's ability to attend to the present. If anything, the opposite occurred. Exploration *enabled* exploitation.

The Coast Guard members I interviewed for my research reported that Long View and Evergreen accomplished this in several ways. At the most explicit level, they identified strategies that the Coast Guard then pursued. Take maritime domain awareness. The scenarios made it clear to Coast Guard leaders that in any plausible future, they would want the ability to identify and track every vessel in U.S. waters. Although this may seem like an obvious need, it's not a capability that the service had in the 1990s. As one retired admiral explained, "Ships could come in 10 miles off or even three miles off the United States' coast, and we might not know it." That was in part because U.S. agencies had no integrated system for gathering and disseminating information.

Even though the Coast Guard didn't have the organizational and technological infrastructure to establish full maritime domain awareness immediately, Long View built consensus about its value among top leadership, which helped the service implement it more quickly after 9/11. In fact, the Coast Guard captain who had managed Evergreen led the interagency effort to develop the first National Strategy for Maritime Security, which ultimately prompted the creation of the Nationwide Automatic Identification System—a sort of transponder system for ships.

The strategies that emerged from the scenario-planning exercises also enabled personnel who participated in them to act with a greater awareness of the service's future needs. For example, the first iteration of Evergreen stressed the importance of building strategic partnerships at home and abroad. With this in mind, one senior Coast Guard leader prepared for threats that might emerge in the Pacific by developing bilateral relationships with island nations there; sharing information, coordinating patrols, and holding joint exercises with counterparts in China, Russia, Canada, South Korea, and Japan; and finding ways to work more closely with other U.S. agencies, from the FBI to the National Oceanic and Atmospheric Administration.

At the most basic level, Long View and Evergreen simply got the service's people to think more about the future. The master chief petty officer of the Coast Guard Reserve described how Evergreen had changed his thinking, citing a recent conversation with a colleague: "He and I were here in my office this morning, talking about, 'Twenty-five years from now, what is the Coast Guard Reserve component going to look like?'" Before taking part in Evergreen, he added, "I just wouldn't understand how to think that way."

Perhaps most interesting, however—and most important in resolving the supposed paradox between exploration and exploitation—is the way that Long View and Evergreen helped participants understand the demands of the past and the future not as competing but as complementary. The exercises changed the very way in which participants thought about time.

Humans tend to conceive of time as linear and unidirectional, as moving from past to present to future, with each time frame discrete. We remember yesterday; we experience today; we anticipate tomorrow. But the best scenario planning embraces a decidedly nonlinear conception of time. That's what Long View and Evergreen did: They took stock of trends in the present, jumped many years into the future, described plausible worlds created by those drivers, worked backward to develop stories about how those worlds had come to pass, and then worked forward again to develop robust strategies. In this model, time circles around on itself, in a constantly evolving feedback cycle between present and future. In a word, it is a loop.

Once participants began to view time as a loop, they understood *thinking about the future* as an essential component of *taking action in the present.* The scenarios gave them a structure that strengthened their ability to be strategic, despite tremendous uncertainty. It became clear that in making decisions, Coast Guard personnel should learn not only from past experience but also from imagined futures.

Getting Started

The prospect of organizing a scenario exercise can intimidate the uninitiated. There are distinct benefits to enlisting one of the individuals, boutique consultancies, or even large firms that specialize in scenarios to provide helpful direction. However, regardless of who runs the process, managers should follow these key guidelines:

Invite the right people to participate

One of the chief purposes of a scenario exercise is to challenge mental models of how the world works. To create the conditions for success, you'll need to bring together participants who have significantly different organizational roles, points of view, and personal experiences. You'll also need people who represent what Kees van der Heijden, one of Wack's successors at Shell, has described as the three powers necessary for any effective conversation about strategy: the power to perceive, the power to think, and the power to act.

Identify assumptions, drivers, and uncertainties

It's important to explicitly articulate the assumptions in your current strategy and what future you expect will result from its implementation. Think of this scenario as your projected scenario—but recognize that it's just one of many possible futures, and focus on determining which assumptions it would be helpful to revisit. Rafael Ramirez, who leads the Oxford Scenarios Programme, advises that in doing this you disaggregate *transactional actors*, which you can influence or control, from *environmental forces*, which you cannot. How might those forces combine to create different possible futures?

Imagine plausible, but dramatically different, futures

This can be the most difficult part of the exercise, particularly for those used to more analytical modes of thinking. Push yourself to imagine what the future will look like in five, 10, or even 20 years—without simply extrapolating from trends in the present. This takes a high degree of creativity and also requires the judgment to distinguish a scenario that, as the Coast Guard puts it, pushes the envelope of plausibility from one that tears it—an inherently subjective task. Good facilitators can both prime the imagination and maintain the guardrails of reality.

Inhabit those futures

Scenario planning is most effective when it's an immersive experience. Creating "artifacts from the future," such as fictional newspaper articles or even video clips, often helps challenge existing mental models. It's also a good idea to disconnect participants from the present, so hold workshops off-site and discourage the use of phones at them.

Isolate strategies that will be useful across multiple possible futures

Form teams to inhabit each of your far-future worlds, and give them this challenge: What should we be doing *now* that would enable us to operate better in that particular future? Create an atmosphere in which even junior participants can put forward ideas without hesitation. Once the groups develop strategies for their worlds, bring them together to compare notes. Look for commonalities, single them out, and identify plans and investments that will make sense across a range of futures.

Implement those strategies

This may sound obvious, but it is the place where most companies fall down. Using scenario planning to devise strategies isn't resource-intensive, but implementing them requires commitment. To couple foresight with action, leaders should set up a formal system in which managers have to explain explicitly how their plans will advance the firm's new strategies. Realistically, foresight will not drive every initiative, but scenario exercises can still be valuable in several ways. First, they can provide participants with a common language to talk about the future. Second, they can build support for an idea within an organization so that when the need for implementation becomes clear, it can move faster. Finally, they can enable participants to act at the unit level, even if the organization as a whole fails to link the present and future as tightly as it should.

Ingrain the process

In the long run you'll reap the greatest value from scenario exercises by establishing an iterative cycle—that is, a process that continually orients your organization toward the future while keeping an eye on the present, and vice versa. This ambidexterity will allow you to thrive under the best of conditions—and it's essential for survival under the worst. Moving in a loop between the present and multiple imagined futures helps you to adjust and update your strategies continually.

This last point is critical. As the current pandemic has made clear, needs and assumptions can change quickly and unpredictably. Preparing for the future demands constant reappraisal. Strategic foresight—the capacity to sense, shape, and adapt to what happens—requires iterative exploration, whether through scenario planning or another method. (See "The Future: A Glossary.) Only by institutionalizing the imaginative process can organizations establish a continual give-and-take between the present and the future. Used dynamically in this way, scenario planning and other tools of strategic foresight allow us to map ever-shifting territory.

Of course, strategic foresight also enables us to identify opportunities and amplifies our ability to seize them. Organizations don't just prepare for the future. They make it. Moments of uncertainty hold great entrepreneurial potential. As Wack once wrote in these pages, "It is precisely in these contexts—not in stable times—that the real opportunities lie to gain competitive advantage through strategy."

It takes strength to stand up against the tyranny of the present and invest in imagination. Strategic foresight makes both possible—and offers leaders a chance for legacy. After all, they will be judged not only by what they do today but by how well they chart a course toward tomorrow.

Originally published in July–August 2020. Reprint R2004B

Leading a New Era of Climate Action

by Andrew Winston

CLIMATE CHANGE IS A GLOBAL EMERGENCY. It's threatening crops, water supplies, infrastructure, and livelihoods. It's damaging the broader economy and company bottom lines *today*, not in some distant future. In recent years AT&T has spent $874 million on repairs after natural disasters that the company ties to climate change. The reinsurance leader Swiss Re has seen large increases in payouts for damage caused by extreme weather events—$2.5 billion more in 2017 than it had predicted—a trend that CEO Christian Mumenthaler attributes to rising global temperatures. If we don't move quickly toward action on climate, says Mark Carney, the Bank of England governor, we'll see company bankruptcies and raise the odds of systemic economic collapse.

Corporate leaders are at last absorbing this; nearly every large company has significant plans to cut carbon emissions and is acting. But given the scale of the crisis and the pace at which it's developing, these efforts are woefully inadequate. Critical UN reports in 2018 and 2019 make two things clear: (1) To avoid *some* of the worst outcomes of climate change, the world must cut carbon emissions by 45% by 2030 and eliminate them entirely by midcentury. (2) Current government plans and commitments are not remotely close to putting us on that path. Emissions are still rising.

Countries, cities, and businesses need to move simultaneously along two paths: reducing emissions dramatically (mitigation) and investing in resilience while planning for vast change (adaptation). My focus here is on mitigation, because adaptation alone—building ever-higher walls to keep out the sea and simply turning up the air-conditioning as the outdoors becomes uninhabitable—won't save us. If we allow climate change to destroy the plant and animal ecosystems we rely on, there will be no replacements. The good news is that business has enormous potential to profitably cut emissions faster and even more.

If the main question for business were still "Which actions will both cut emissions and create short-term value?" we know the answer: slash carbon in energy-intensive industries and in operations, transportation, and buildings; buy lots of renewable energy, which is strategically smart because it has been competitive with fossil fuels for years; reduce waste, particularly in critical sectors such as food and agriculture; expand the use of circular business models that minimize resource use; embed climate change metrics in corporate systems and key performance indicators, and more. Again, most companies have begun to take advantage of these "basic" opportunities and will accelerate adoption as they see the payoff grow. So let's assume that they will continue down this path. Then what?

Given the urgency, we must ask a different, and harder, question: "What are *all* the things business can possibly do with its vast resources?" What capital—financial, human, brand, and political—can companies bring to bear?

Drawing on 20 years of consulting to global corporations and working on climate change issues, I see three actions that companies must now focus on to drive deeper change:

- using political influence to demand aggressive climate policies around the world

- empowering suppliers, customers, and employees to drive change

- rethinking investments and business models to eliminate waste and carbon throughout the economy

These actions may feel unnatural to some executives if they appear to put larger interests ahead of immediate shareholder profits.

Idea in Brief

Climate change is a global emergency that threatens crops, water supplies, infrastructure, and livelihoods. It's damaging the economy and company bottom lines. Most large companies are cutting carbon emissions, but given the scale of the crisis, these efforts are sadly inadequate. Companies need to mobilize, says Andrew Winston, to deal with this unprecedented global problem. He draws on 20 years of consulting for global corporations to recommend three actions:

- Use political influence to demand aggressive climate policies.

- Empower suppliers, customers, and employees to drive change.

- Rethink investments and business models to eliminate waste and carbon.

But the tide is turning on the very idea of shareholder primacy. The roughly 200 largest multinationals based in the United States recently declared, through the Business Roundtable, that they will no longer focus solely on shareholders or on the short run. We are at a pivotal moment as the climate crisis propels companies' growing sense of social purpose. The result, I believe, is the will needed to finally achieve this deeper change.

What's in It for Us?

Before I dig into the three areas of change, it's fair to ask why a company would commit to such challenging and possibly risky initiatives. One argument is macro/societal and the other is microeconomic. The former is straightforward: Companies need healthy people and a viable planet; with expensive runaway climate change on the horizon, they have an economic imperative and a moral responsibility to do everything they can to ensure a thriving world. As Unilever's former CEO Paul Polman says, "Business simply can't be a bystander in a system that gives it life in the first place." And let's not forget that even as they pursue their own self-interest, executives sometimes just do what they believe is the right thing, which may or may not pay off—from ceasing to sell assault weapons at Dick's Sporting Goods and Walmart to funding

The Big Idea: Mobilizing on Climate

"Leading a New Era of Climate Action" is the lead article of HBR's **The Big Idea: Mobilizing on Climate.** Read the rest of the series at hbr.org/climate:

- "Tough Business Questions About the Climate Crisis," by Andy Robinson
- "What Do People Really Believe About Climate Change?" by Gretchen Gavett
- "Your Company's Next Leader on Climate Is . . . the CFO," by Laura Palmeiro and Delphine Gibassier
- "The New Business of Garbage," by Laura Amico
- "A Better Way to Talk About the Climate Crisis," by Gretchen Gavett
- "Is Your Trade Group Blocking Climate Action?" by Sheldon Whitehouse

by Apple and Microsoft of programs to reduce homelessness in their neighborhoods.

The microeconomic argument, however, is often overlooked. Stakeholders, particularly customers and employees, have increasingly high standards for the companies they buy from and work for. Business customers are demanding more sustainability performance from suppliers every year. Consumers are seeking out sustainable brands (50% of consumer packaged goods growth from 2013 to 2018 came from sustainability-marketed products), and Deloitte's global surveys show that up to 87% of the under-40 crowd—the Millennials who will make up 75% of the global workforce in five years—believes that a company's success should be measured in more than just financial terms. And nine in 10 members of Gen Z agree that companies have a responsibility to engage with environmental and social issues.

Employees are now directly pressuring their companies to do more on climate, particularly in the tech sector. In direct and public appeals, Google employees have asked their executives to cut ties to climate deniers, and Microsoft's employees staged a walkout in protest of the company's "complicity in the climate crisis." At Amazon more than 8,700 workers have signed an open letter to CEO Jeff Bezos with a list

Alarming forecast: current climate policies are grossly inadequate

To hold global warming to 1.5° Celsius above preindustrial levels and prevent the worst impacts of climate change, the world must cut carbon emissions to zero by midcentury. Yet emissions are still rising, and under existing policies reductions won't begin to approach what's needed. If we stay on the current path, temperatures will probably increase by about 3° C, with catastrophic effects.

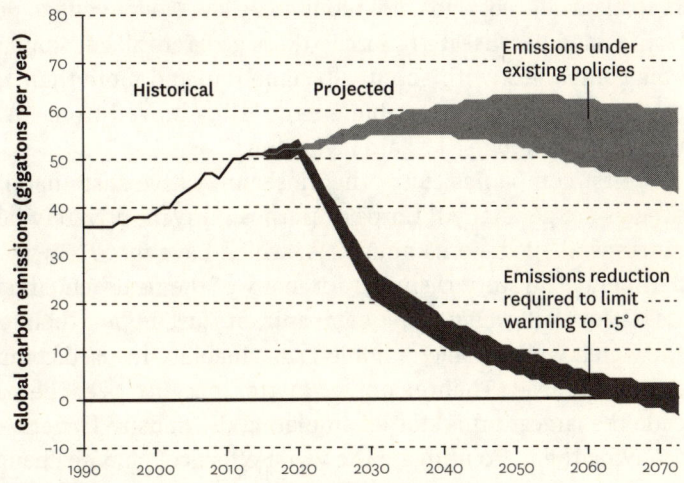

Note: Band widths represent high and low emissions estimates.

Source: Climate Action Tracker

of demands, including developing a plan to get to zero emissions and eliminating donations to climate-denying legislators. Their efforts clearly played a part in pushing Bezos to announce large ambitions to be carbon neutral by 2040 and to buy 100,000 electric vehicles.

Because of pressure like this, along with increasingly dire warnings from climate scientists and global bodies including the UN, corporate efforts to reduce emissions have become table stakes—something any company *must* do to earn respect from employees and customers. And what is common and accepted practice, regardless of the short-term ROI, can sometimes shift very quickly. Consider that nobody could prove the value of diversity and inclusion when companies first dove into that issue. Now we have good data—but the norms changed first.

I've seen firsthand how this can play out on sustainability issues. Nearly six years ago, in my book The Big Pivot, I advocated setting science-based emissions-reduction goals. Virtually no companies were doing that then, and I argued with many who wondered why a company would set a goal not required by law. Now, owing to peer pressure—and because it's rational—those goals are all but standard for big companies, with about 750 signed up and more than 200 committing to 100% renewable energy. They moved from "Why would we?" to "You're a laggard if you don't."

The first companies to try the most innovative sustainability strategies are generally B Corps or purpose-driven, privately held businesses like Patagonia and IKEA, which have more leeway to experiment. The story is similar for many of the next-gen climate ideas I lay out below: Big public companies are just dipping their toes in the water, while smaller, nimbler, sustainability-focused companies take the lead. Their examples matter, because over the past decade the largest firms started emulating the midsize leaders—or just buying them. To mitigate the worst effects of climate change, more companies need to follow, and fast.

Let's return now to the three broad activities that every company, big or small, must undertake.

1. Use Political Influence for Climate Good

Given the scale of the climate crisis, business alone can't solve it. But business does have a powerful tool beyond its own practices and products: extensive and deep tendrils in the halls of political power. All over the world, but especially in market economies, companies have enormous influence over governments and politicians. Through large campaign donations and—in the United States after the Supreme Court case *Citizens United*—nearly unlimited spending on political ads, the corporate agenda gets an outsize voice in society. How can and should companies use that power?

Business's government relations have traditionally been aimed at reshaping or fighting regulations. But over the past few years many companies have, at least on the surface, been supporting some climate policy. Hundreds of multinationals with operations in the U.S. have signed statements such as "We Are Still In" and the recent "United for the Paris Agreement" to let the world know that they will cut emissions in keeping with the Paris Climate Accords and that they want the U.S. government to stay aboard, despite announcements that it would not. Another group of large companies called for the world to hold warming to just 1.5 degrees Celsius. Signatories came from every corner of the planet: Sweden (Electrolux), Japan (ASICS), India (Mahindra Group), Switzerland (Nestlé), Germany (SAP), and many other places and sectors.

But statements alone are inadequate. Companies must lobby for the policies that will lead to a low-carbon future, and senior executives need to show up in person. Without collective government action, we have little chance of avoiding the direst outcomes of climate change. One industry—fossil fuels—has had a dominant, decades-long influence on climate policies in world capitals, and for good reason: Policies aimed at reducing emissions pose an existential threat to the business. Companies in every other sector must grasp that climate change, which may spin out of control without enlightened policies, is an existential threat to *their* businesses.

For the most part, non–fossil fuel companies engage only in occasional special lobbying days organized by the likes of Ceres, the American Sustainable Business Council, and Business Climate Leaders. Those events are important, of course, but even the groups themselves acknowledge that the number of big companies with a consistent climate-action focus is small. As Joe Britton, a former chief of staff for U.S. Senator Martin Heinrich, told me, these temporary "fly-ins" are better than nothing, but they are overshadowed by the daily swarm of fossil fuel lobbyists. In response, Britton left his position to create a new lobbying organization, with the help of other Capitol Hill insiders, to deploy a fuller and more constant political message to Congress on climate.

There's also a major disconnect between what companies say about their commitments to fight climate change and what those who represent them—the trade associations or even their own government relations people—actually push for. As transparency increases, companies should worry about any gap between their sustainability commitments and their lobbying. An NGO, Australia's Lobby Watch, is calling out the mining giant BHP and others for such disconnects. And the UK-based influencemap.org is tracking corporate lobbying activity on climate at hundreds of companies and publicly highlighting hypocrisy.

For leaders, aggressive climate lobbying is not just about appearances; it can create advantage. If 100% of your energy comes from renewables, a price on carbon won't affect your own cost structure much. And if you make products or provide services that help reduce emissions, you benefit from tighter carbon controls. That's surely one reason that Germany's Siemens, with a portfolio of products that improve energy efficiency, states that its top political engagement goal is "combating Climate Change."

Hugh Welsh, the president for North America at DSM, a large Dutch company that offers nutrition, health, and sustainable-living products and solutions, can attest to this. He has worked for years to bring a business voice on climate to the halls of political power. Welsh says he does this for two reasons: principles and pragmatism. About the former, he says, "Over 10 years as president, I've developed political capital. I can use that just for strategic things for the business, but I can also use that to improve the world." About the latter, he notes that DSM serves several sustainability-focused product markets, so a proactive role on sustainability and climate policy fits its strategy.

When Welsh makes the case to skeptical executives, leaders, and trade groups—such as the recalcitrant U.S. Chamber of Commerce, with which he worked for two years to flip its position on climate—he says, "If you don't evolve your position, you'll be on the wrong side of history . . . your partners and customers will leave in droves."

Rising temperatures, rising risks: flooding cities

If the global temperature were to increase by . . .

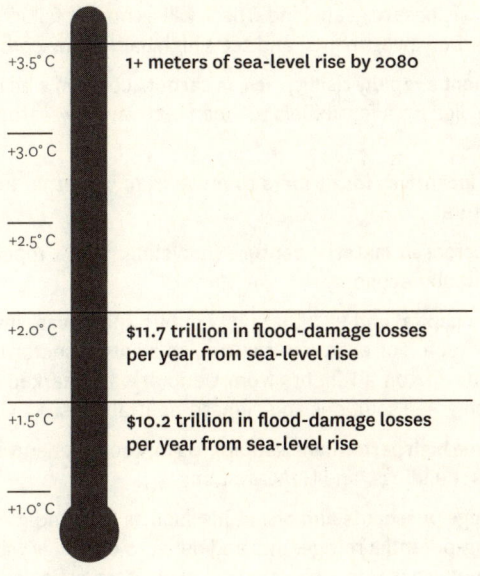

+3.5° C	1+ meters of sea-level rise by 2080
+3.0° C	
+2.5° C	
+2.0° C	$11.7 trillion in flood-damage losses per year from sea-level rise
+1.5° C	$10.2 trillion in flood-damage losses per year from sea-level rise
+1.0° C	

Source: World Resources Institute

So what policies should companies advocate? To move the world to a low-carbon future, we need bold plans in a few key areas: pricing carbon and mobilizing capital to shift to low-carbon systems; rapidly raising performance standards and phasing out old technologies for big energy users like cars and buildings; and enabling transparency and efforts to reduce human suffering.

These priorities apply in most geographies, but of course policy formation and the relationship between business and government vary widely across countries. Approaches in command-and-control economies must vary from those in sprawling capitalist systems.

Policies may take years to have an effect, so these efforts must be made soon. It's time for companies to use their substantial political

Climate Policies Companies Should Fight For

A LONG LIST OF POSSIBLE GOVERNMENT POLICIES could create the conditions for rapid emissions reductions. But the following are probably the most important for business to get behind. These will fix market failures, shift capital toward low-carbon investments, and set a high bar for low-carbon products.

Implement a rapidly rising price on carbon, coupled with massive shifts in subsidies from fossil fuels to clean tech and low-carbon production methods.

Create incentives for farmers to move from industrial to regenerative agriculture.

Fund increased material capture (recycling, reuse, repair) to encourage a circular economy.

Mobilize capital and R&D that pulls public and private investment into cleaner tech. For example, the Danish aviation sector has proposed a climate tax on all flights from Denmark, earmarked for a fund to research green solutions and climate-neutral fuels.

Introduce high performance standards for the big energy users, including cars, buildings, and HVAC systems.

Encourage phaseouts and phase-ins such as by mandating low-global-warming-potential refrigerants and net-zero buildings with renewables and banning gas-guzzlers. Some countries have set a date for stopping the sale of internal combustion engines: Norway by 2025, Sweden and Denmark by 2030, and France and Sri Lanka by 2040.

Prioritize transparency through, for example, the Task Force on Climate-related Financial Disclosures, which provides guidelines for companies reporting their material risks from climate change, and product labels with carbon-footprint information, much like the calorie and nutrition counts on food labels.

Fund resources for adaptation, such as resilience planning in cities, the relocation of citizens, and retraining for those from older sectors that will rapidly decline.

influence to proactively support laws that make high-carbon products and choices more expensive, mobilize capital toward a clean economy, support systems change, and help deal with adaptation and the human costs of shifts to clean technology.

2. Leverage Stakeholder Relationships

At the same time, companies should wield their other superpower: vast influence over value chain partners and deep connections to their customers and employees. Big consumer products companies like P&G and Unilever often rightly brag that they serve billions of people every day. More than 275 million people visit a Walmart every week. Companies employ hundreds of millions of us. And with nearly $33 trillion in revenues across the *Fortune* Global 500 alone, it's safe to assume that many trillions go to suppliers. Imagine if companies used those touch points, their buying power, and all their communications and advertising clout to catalyze change across business and society.

Suppliers

In recent years corporations have ratcheted up the pressure on their suppliers to operate more sustainably. Big buyers increasingly want to see progress—backed up by data—in a supplier's carbon footprint, resource use, human rights and labor performance, and much more. General Mills, Kellogg, IKEA, and Hewlett Packard Enterprise have all set science-based carbon goals for their suppliers. Others, including GSK, H&M, Toyota, and Schneider Electric, have committed to carbon neutrality or negativity (eliminating more carbon than is produced) in their entire value chains by 2040 or 2050.

Commitments like these are becoming the norm. But what else is possible? What are boundary-pushing companies doing to drive change? I see future supply-chain climate leadership in three key areas: providing capital, driving innovation and collaboration, and using purchasing power to choose suppliers on the basis of emissions performance.

Financial assistance and capital. Making a business more sustainable is profitable, but it may still require investments and capital. Companies that ask suppliers to change how they do business can help, especially with smaller players. For example, in mid-2018, after achieving 100% renewable energy in its own operations, Apple launched the China Clean Energy Fund, a joint pool of $300 million

---

Rising temperatures, rising risks: food shortages

If the global temperature were to increase by . . .

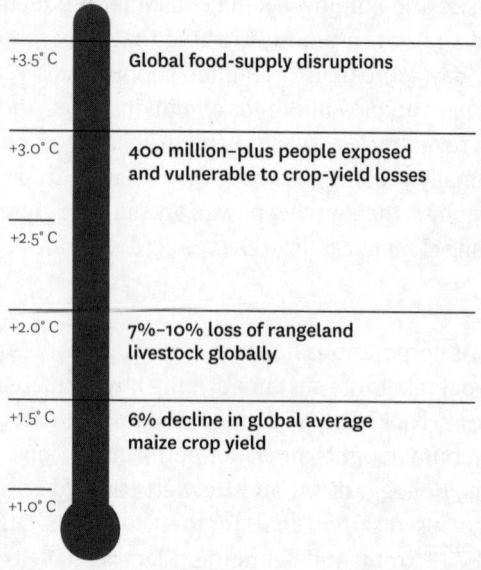

+3.5° C	Global food-supply disruptions
+3.0° C	400 million–plus people exposed and vulnerable to crop-yield losses
+2.5° C	
+2.0° C	7%–10% loss of rangeland livestock globally
+1.5° C	6% decline in global average maize crop yield
+1.0° C	

Source: World Resources Institute

---

to help suppliers buy one gigawatt of renewable energy, and the fund's first big wind farms went up last year. Similarly, IKEA recently committed €100 million to help first-tier suppliers make the shift. In another innovative approach, an industrial company I work with, Ingersoll Rand (better known by its brands Thermo King and Trane), financed a large renewable energy project and then invited suppliers to offset their emissions by buying portions of the energy production. And beyond encouraging renewables, some leaders, such as Levi's and Walmart, have worked with HSBC and other banks to provide lower interest rates to suppliers that score well on sustainability performance.

Joint innovation. I also recently watched the head of procurement at Ingersoll Rand tell hundreds of suppliers that his company would no longer choose vendors on the basis of pricing and quality alone. Now, he said, suppliers would need to innovate *with* the company to make its products more energy- and carbon-efficient. This is a great way to drive value chain innovation, but sectorwide collaboration can have an even bigger impact.

Consider that Walmart and Target, which are traditionally competitors, worked together with the NGO Forum for the Future (on whose board I serve) to create the Beauty and Personal Care Sustainability Project—a creative attempt at improving the environmental and social footprint of all the products we put on our bodies. They brought together big CPG companies such as P&G and Unilever and their chemical suppliers to rethink ingredients, packaging, and more to reduce health and environmental impacts. Apple has dived deep into its supply chain to make its ubiquitous tech products lower-carbon, including through a joint venture with Rio Tinto and Alcoa to develop and commercialize an aluminum-smelting process with vastly lower greenhouse gas emissions and lower costs.

Purchasing power. For years many companies have agreed to work with lagging suppliers to improve their sustainability performance. But the world can no longer afford to wait for slow adopters. Companies should cut them loose and shift their purchasing dollars toward the low-carbon leaders—which are often the best-run suppliers anyway. VF Corporation, the home of brands such as Vans and The North Face, stopped buying leather from Brazil because government policy there was encouraging Amazon rainforest destruction.

Retailers should make carbon performance a buying priority. Mainstream mega-retailers like Walmart and Target have pressured suppliers for years to make their offerings more sustainable, but they could do much more to support those that are best at reducing emissions in their operations or through their products. They could, for example, permanently (not just on Earth Day) devote endcaps or special promotion areas—their highest-value real estate—to drive business to the lowest-carbon-emitting suppliers while satisfying growing customer demand for green products. It's a win-win, but it's not normal practice yet.

Customers

The core thing companies are doing—and must continue to do—is helping customers reduce carbon emissions by developing and offering products that produce fewer emissions throughout their life cycles. We're seeing great innovation, and customer buy-in, for lower-footprint products in the biggest carbon-emitting sectors: electric vehicles in transportation; efficient heating, cooling, and lighting in buildings; and tasty alternative proteins in food and agriculture.

Manufacturers and retailers are also working to increase the use of recycled materials and reduce the amount of material used in packaging—all the way to zero in some cases. A group of British retailers, for example, has teamed up to change how some products leave the store. Consumers can fill their own bags and jars from bins of dry goods (grains, beans, nuts, and so on), laundry detergent, and shampoo. Some commercial products are trying to go even further: After making each tile of its prototype carbon-negative flooring, Interface explains, "there is less carbon dioxide in the atmosphere than if it had not been manufactured in the first place."

But businesses need to make products like these mainstream and then go beyond the direct impacts of their products on customers to drive deeper change. Here are three possible ways forward:

Help customers use less and mobilize. The two most aggressive actions companies can take with consumers are encouraging them to reduce consumption and engaging them in climate activism. Zurich-based Freitag, which makes bags from recycled materials, lets customers create a new look by switching bags with other customers. And Patagonia (always a radical company) is teaching its customers how to repair its clothes so that they don't need to buy new items. These companies may risk selling less, but they're building trusted brands with a loyal following. And discouraging consumption hasn't hurt Patagonia in the least: Sales have quadrupled

Rising temperatures, rising risks: nature's collapse

If the global temperature were to increase by . . .

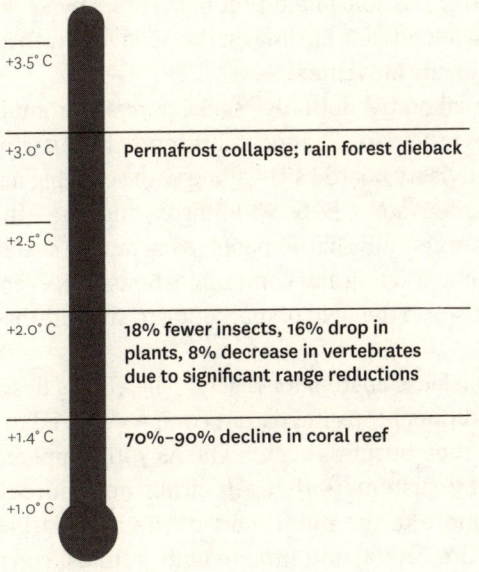

+3.5° C

+3.0° C Permafrost collapse; rain forest dieback

+2.5° C

+2.0° C 18% fewer insects, 16% drop in plants, 8% decrease in vertebrates due to significant range reductions

+1.4° C 70%–90% decline in coral reef

+1.0° C

Source: World Resources Institute

over the past decade, reaching an estimated $1 billion. Going further, the company is using the trust it has built to mobilize consumers, through its Patagonia Action Works initiative, to engage with grassroots environmental groups in Europe and the United States.

Use communications to educate and inspire consumers. Companies can make more-effective use of two channels in driving climate discussions: packaging and advertising. How? The Swedish oat drink brand Oatly, for example, reports product carbon emissions on its packages and points consumers to information on the climate benefits of eating plant-based products. Ben & Jerry's used the packaging and launch of an ice cream flavor, Save Our Swirled, to raise awareness about the Paris Climate Accords in 2015. IKEA surveyed more than 14,000 customers in 14 countries to understand their attitudes and how best to motivate climate action through advertising; the resulting framework is designed to guide its communications. In the fall of 2019 the household products company Seventh Generation donated advertising airtime on the *Today* show to help promote the Youth Climate Movement.

A new collaborative initiative seeks to make promotional activities like these the norm. Launched recently by Sustainable Brands (on whose advisory board I sit)—along with some big names such as PepsiCo, Nestlé Waters, P&G, SC Johnson, and Visa—the Brands for Good program commits participants to encourage sustainable living through their marketing and communications and, even more ambitious, to transform the field of marketing to support that goal.

Choose business customers wisely. The efforts described above focus on traditional consumers. But companies need to direct equal attention to their business customers. As with suppliers, they must stop enabling customers that are either not addressing climate change or, more to the point, part of the high-carbon economy. Banks, venture capital and private equity funds, consulting companies, legal firms, and other service providers should ask tough questions about whom they're supporting. Helping companies be "better" at extracting or burning carbon-based fuels is actively moving the world in the wrong direction, and it dwarfs any carbon reduction a service business pursues in its own operations.

In the investment world, a movement to divest from fossil fuels is taking off, spearheaded by a group of investors with $11 trillion in assets. Norway's $1 trillion sovereign wealth fund is likewise dumping investments in many oil and gas companies.

Other service companies, such as consulting giants and law firms, that still work with carbon-intensive industries should be helping them make the permanent pivot necessary to survive. That means helping fossil fuel companies sunset their core business over the next few decades and completely shift their portfolios and business models toward clean options. Tech companies have to do some hard thinking as well. One of the reasons Amazon's employees rebelled was the company's announcement that its cloud business would help oil and gas companies accelerate exploration. Stakeholders will continue to ask probing questions about what companies stand for and whom they support—and companies will have to have an answer.

Employees

In the battle for talent, especially for Millennials and Gen Z, companies must prove that they are good citizens. Surveys consistently show that people under 40 want to work for employers that share their values. As Unilever's sustainable living plan gained steam in the mid-2010s, the company became the most sought-after employer in its sector. Top executives I've worked with at Unilever cite its sustainability leadership as key in attracting and retaining talent. The benefit flows both ways: Companies need their employees' commitment and buy-in to achieve their sustainability goals.

To reinforce this relationship, companies must build sustainability and climate action into their regular incentive structures and systems— that is, pay everyone from the C-suite on down to cut carbon. They are secretive about the exact percentages, but the most committed companies I've seen tie at least a quarter of bonuses to sustainability key performance indicators (KPIs). It's time to increase that.

Can companies go even further and proactively support their employees' values by helping them drive change in the world around them? Some organizations already do. During the 2018 U.S. election, more than 100 of them, including Walmart, Levi Strauss, The Gap, Southwest Airlines, Kaiser Permanente, and Lyft, joined the Time to Vote initiative, giving employees time off to be good citizens. Some even encourage direct climate activism. Having identified the "climate emergency" as a top employee concern, the $1 billion cosmetics retailer Lush closed 200 shops in the U.S. to allow employees to join global climate marches last September. A Lush representative told me that during Canadian marches the company also shuttered 50 shops and offices for 20 manufacturing and support teams.

Atlassian, the fast-growing Australian enterprise software company with a $30 billion market cap, also encourages employees to

Rising temperatures, rising risks: heat waves

If the global temperature were to increase by . . .

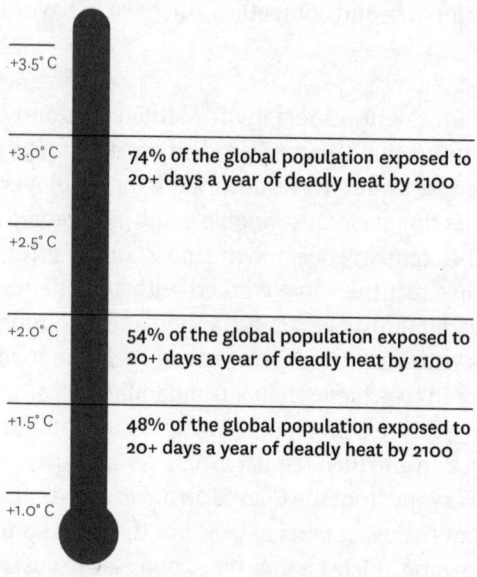

+3.5° C

+3.0° C — 74% of the global population exposed to 20+ days a year of deadly heat by 2100

+2.5° C

+2.0° C — 54% of the global population exposed to 20+ days a year of deadly heat by 2100

+1.5° C — 48% of the global population exposed to 20+ days a year of deadly heat by 2100

+1.0° C

Note: According to research published in *Nature Climate Change*, "deadly heat" is the threshold beyond which air temperatures, humidity, and other factors can be lethal.

Source: World Resources Institute

become climate activists. As the company's cofounder Mike Cannon-Brookes wrote in his blunt blog "Don't @#$% the planet," Atlassian gives employees a week each year to volunteer for charity, and they can now use the time to join marches and strikes. He wants them to "go further and volunteer their time to other not-for-profit groups with a focus on climate."

Employees want to work for a company that stands for something. But they increasingly also want the freedom to express what *they* stand for. So ask them what they care about—especially younger and newer employees—and help them live their values.

3. Rethinking the Business

Flexing political muscle and reconceiving stakeholder relationships must happen quickly. But it is also time to think big, to look for new possibilities, and to question core assumptions about consumption and growth in the economy—that is, to go far beyond simply slashing energy use and buying renewables. Today the possibilities are broad, with everything from reducing food waste to developing circular business models falling under the umbrella of "climate strategy." Now is the right time to think critically and creatively about how *all* products and services in every sector are created and used and to squeeze carbon out of every step in the value chain. Some of this is tactical—for example, working with suppliers or customers to reduce their emissions, as discussed. But at the strategic level it can mean rethinking the company's investments and business models entirely. Here are some ways to do just that, focused on two key areas.

Risk and investments

Companies deploy capital and make investment decisions in multiple ways. With some important changes in how they think about financing and investment, much more capital could flow to low-carbon activities.

Consider the idea of return on investment. In most companies, to get internal funding, a project must achieve a predetermined rate of return (or hurdle rate) that will pay off relatively quickly. This approach to ROI is flawed. It generally measures the "R" in straight cash, without allowing for more-strategic or intangible value. It's also agnostic as to whether the investment moves the company down a more sustainable path. We need to use this tool differently to shift to low-carbon investment choices.

Smart tweaks to two internal processes—capital expenditures and hurdle rates—can do a lot of good. J. M. Huber, a family-owned business that manufactures nature-based ingredients for the food and personal care industries along with components in home building, developed a more holistic approach to optimizing capital deployment. The chief sustainability officer and the CFO worked together to

Rising temperatures, rising risks: water uncertainty

If the global temperature were to increase by . . .

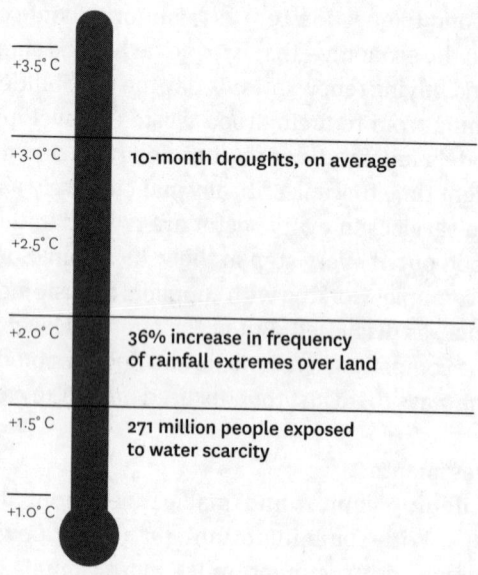

+3.5° C

+3.0° C — 10-month droughts, on average

+2.5° C

+2.0° C — 36% increase in frequency
of rainfall extremes over land

+1.5° C — 271 million people exposed
to water scarcity

+1.0° C

Note: According to the NOAA, "extreme rainfall" can be loosely defined as a month's worth of rain for a given region falling in a single day.

Source: World Resources Institute

shift the capex process to factor in intangible benefits such as community engagement, customer perceptions, employee attraction and retention, and business resiliency (for example, solar array projects that insulate the business from fossil fuel energy price shocks).

Companies should set their hurdle rates more strategically and allow some investments more leeway, with a strong bias toward funding carbon-reducing projects. If, for example, constructing an energy-efficient building—one that will save money and carbon over its lifetime—costs more up front or requires more than a few years to pay off, isn't it still a smart investment on a 40-year asset?

Another wise investment shift involves levying an internal carbon price on companies' own operations to encourage emissions reduction. More than 1,400 organizations now use internal pricing in some way, but the norm is to use "shadow" prices with no money changing hands. That approach isn't strong enough. Early leaders like Microsoft, Disney, and LVMH have been collecting *real* money from divisions or functions related to their emissions. That "tax" revenue is reinvested in energy efficiency, renewables, or offset projects such as tree planting. All companies should use this strategy to help fund low-carbon projects and to prepare the business as government-imposed carbon taxes become more common.

A more recent strategy is to use financing tools such as green bonds, now a $200 billion market, in which the proceeds from bond purchases go to environmental and climate projects. The Italian energy group ENEL is trying something a bit different, issuing a bond tied to a KPI measuring the company's performance against the UN's Sustainable Development Goals. If ENEL misses its target of increasing renewable energy to 55% of its installed capacity, it will pay 25 basis points more to bondholders. Although the funds raised are not tied to a specific use, as they are with conventional green bonds, the instrument clearly supports emissions reduction.

Perhaps the biggest move a company can make is to rethink where to place its R&D bets. In a telling seismic shift, Daimler announced that it would no longer invest in research on internal combustion engines and would put billions toward electric vehicles instead. And the CEO of Nestlé, Mark Schneider, spoke recently about investing in plant-based proteins, which have a *much* smaller carbon footprint than conventionally produced meat, saying, "A Swiss franc we spend developing the burger is a burden to this quarter's profits. Next year or the year after, it will come back to us if we do our job right." Seeing returns on a fast-growing new market within a year or two sounds like a good deal.

New business models

The level of carbon reduction that the Intergovernmental Panel on Climate Change says is required to head off catastrophic warming—cutting emissions in half by 2030 and to zero by 2050—is daunting. Everything discussed here will move us much more quickly, but some fundamental changes are needed in how we think about products, services, and consumption. Current business models and delivery methods can lock us into more material- and energy-intensive pathways. And some sectors, the most carbon-intensive, will need to exit core businesses.

Consider Philips Lighting, which launched a "light as a service" model, through which business customers pay Philips to install and manage their lighting rather than purchase a lighting system themselves. This flips Phillips's traditional model on its head: Instead of trying to sell as many bulbs as possible, under this program, the company manages the provision of light as frugally as it can, using longer-lasting, more-efficient products that slash material and energy use. In a larger-scale transformation, the energy company Ørsted—formerly known as Danish Oil & Natural Gas—anticipated the decarbonization of the global economy and began pivoting from its core business a decade ago. It has since sold off most of its fossil fuel assets and has become the world's largest builder of offshore wind farms. And just a few years ago, the idea that meat-based McDonald's and Burger King would both be selling plant-based "burgers" seemed far-fetched. But they, like Ørsted, maybe thinking strategically about what the coming low-carbon economy means for their business.

The Next Level of Action

There's no doubt that companies are doing a lot on climate, including cutting emissions and setting aggressive carbon goals for operations, supply chains, and their innovation agendas. But it's not enough. The science is getting away from us, and we're losing the relatively stable planetary temperature range that allowed us to build our society over the past 10,000 years. Companies have many levers to pull to truly change business as usual, but most remain stuck in old thinking. Climate action is usually focused on incremental change. And even when they're setting a big goal like going to all-renewable energy, companies have waited until every project makes money quickly. Now they need to mobilize *all* corporate assets, hard *and* soft, to tackle this shared, unprecedented problem at the scale it requires.

Next-gen climate actions, as they become an expected part of business, will create significant longterm value. They will help companies build closer, lasting connections with key stakeholders; create clear and consistent regulatory environments that enable more sustainable practices that lower costs; and drive deeper, more-disruptive (or what I call *heretical*) innovation. Throw in the substantial intangible value—employee attraction and loyalty, lowered risk in supply chain, resilience, license to operate, societal relevance, and preparation for a very different future—and you have a powerful business case.

But it's also well past time to recognize that aggressive climate action is necessary if humanity is to survive and thrive. Business and society won't succeed unless and until we do all we can to tackle climate change.

Your Company's Next Leader on Climate Is . . . the CFO

by Laura Palmeiro and Delphine Gibassier

If your chief financial officer is the last person you would think of to take charge on climate change, think again. Today, smart organizations are shifting their sustainability responsibilities toward the finance function.

There are several reasons for this change. First is the basic math, which falls largely within a CFO's purview. Mitigating and adapting to climate change will require close to $1 trillion in investments per year through 2030 for the economy as a whole, and is also expected to put at risk between $4.2 trillion and $43 trillion of tradable stock exchange assets by the end of the century, depending on the level of planetary warming. (The latter number is for a world that has warmed by 6 degrees Celsius.)

Second, cutting greenhouse gas (GHG) emissions leads to cost savings. If you cut emissions, you cut energy, which is a massive organizational cost—something CFOs pay close attention to. Third, because investors are pushing to make climate-safe investments, they want climate risks to be integrated within corporate financial disclosures. Finally, the business opportunities for climate change solutions are blooming. According to Chartered Professional Accountants of Canada, "As creators, enablers, preservers and reporters of sustainable value, accountants can make their organizations' adaptation efforts more effective." Taken together, these shifts are leading finance teams to include what were formerly called "nonfinancials" in their daily jobs.

CFO leadership on climate change is starting to pay off. For example, Adnams, a British brewery, recently saw an increase in the base cost of beer because hot summers were affecting barley production. To solve the problem, the CFO was able to offset these higher costs by looking at energy and water savings. The CFO of Mars, Claus Aagaard, has talked about how the company's sustainability plan allowed it to capitalize on cost savings within two years.

Through our research, our corporate experience at Danone, and our work with the UN Global Compact, we have determined four key ways in which sustainability is being centralized in the finance function—ways every corporate leader should be aware of.

Financial Tools Are Becoming More Green

Increasingly, we've seen finance teams greening more of their tools. What does this look like? Companies such as SSE or the Coca-Cola Hellenic Bottling Company, for example, have implemented "green CAPEX [capital expenditure]" systems. These structures, which involve small changes in investment decisions (like including an internal price on carbon emissions or loosening the payback period for investment decisions), have allowed climate change–friendly investments to take place on a larger scale.

Even more significant, Microsoft now has an internal carbon market co-designed by the finance and sustainability teams. Thanks to a carbon fee paid by subsidiaries based on the level of their GHG emissions—incentivizing them to cut their emissions—Microsoft has a carbon fund that fuels climate change–related investments, allowing more significant and global investments to be made. On January 16, 2020, Microsoft made a historic announcement, backed by its CFO, to become carbon negative by 2030 and remove their historical carbon emissions by 2050.

In fact, more than 600 organizations say they now use carbon pricing, for a number of different reasons, among them to inform procurement and R&D decisions, help suppliers transition to a low-carbon world, pay bonuses, or help with long-term investments. In another change, Danone has started rewarding strong group performance by connecting incentives to climate change performance based on annual CDP scores.

Finally, following the integration of climate change within management control systems, corporations have started to measure GHG emissions like they measure their financials. Oracle has used what it calls "environmental accounting and reporting" to capture and transform GHG emissions from the company's portfolio of 600 buildings across more than 70 countries. This has led to significant cost savings, because accurate data is being collected quickly. Even the small French company Saveurs et Vie, which produces food baskets for the elderly, has asked its enterprise resource planning system provider to allow it to automate carbon footprinting.

Finance Teams, Collaborations, and Roles Are Evolving

Changes in finance and accounting departments are increasingly visible within not only the tools but also the teams. Ørsted, a wind-power company based in Denmark, has a full-time environmental, social, and governance (ESG) accounting team made up of four employees. The UK-based energy provider SSE has a full-time sustainability accountant in-house. Since 2013, Unilever has had a finance director for sustainability, who is in charge of developing an understanding of sustainability in finance, integrating sustainability into finance reporting, and developing best practices.

These company-specific examples are giving way to larger collaborations, too. The CFO Leadership Network, created in 2010 by Accounting for Sustainability in the UK, recently developed two Canadian and U.S. charters.

Some are rethinking the traditional CFO role altogether. In 2018, the Institute of Management Accountants published the first study on the emergence of sustainability CFOs (coauthored by one of us, Delphine), demonstrating the need for specific hybridized competencies between finance and sustainability to answer today's challenges. This research uncovered new competencies these leaders need to have, including developing natural capital profit and loss accounts, identifying the cost of key externalities, and understanding the value created through intangibles. Going further, Mervyn King (who is credited with the birth of "integrated reporting" in South Africa) developed the concept of a chief value officer in a 2016 book. And in North America, Manulife brought on a sustainability accounting director as a new kind of role.

Rules and Regulations Are Changing Rapidly

Your CFO will also need to adapt to shifting financial accounting rules that address climate change–related risks and opportunities. The biggest changes stem from December 2015, when the Financial Stability Board, an international body that monitors and makes recommendations about the global financial system, established the Task Force on Climate-related Financial Disclosures (TCFD) "to develop a set of voluntary, consistent disclosure recommendations for use by companies in providing information to investors, lenders and insurance underwriters about their climate-related financial risks." The new TCFD recommendations were released in June 2017 and included the suggestion that climate-related financial disclosures be made within mainstream annual financial filings and under governance processes similar to those for public disclosures.

What does this mean in practice? For one, all disclosures, including climate-related risks, climate metrics, and targets, should be reviewed by a company's CFO, audit committee, or both. Companies also should face the future risks of their business models through scenario analysis.

In November 2019, the International Accounting Standards Board (IASB), whose mission is to develop accounting standards for financial markets around the world, published the report "IFRS Standards and Climate-Related Disclosures," which recommended that companies address material environmental and societal issues and, more specifically, issues driven by investor pressure to disclose climate-related risks. (This was especially significant because the IASB usually does not mention climate change in accounting standards or briefings.) We expect recommendations like those from the TCFD and the IASB to continue.

The Financial Markets Increasingly Require a Focus on Climate

The financial markets are driving CFOs to look seriously at climate change. For example, the investor initiative Climate Action 100+, representing more than 370 investors with over $35 trillion in assets collectively, is urging 100 systemically important emitters to curb emissions, improve governance, and strengthen climate-related financial disclosures. Other initiatives, such as the climate benchmarks published by the European Union or the UN's Net Zero Asset Owner Alliance, are shifting the investment world into climate-ready financing. And in his annual letter to CEOs, BlackRock's Larry Fink emphasized that "the evidence on climate risk is compelling investors to reassess core assumptions about modern finance." Ultimately, Fink concluded that "climate risk is investment risk" and is alerting clients that BlackRock is centering its investment approach around sustainability.

Another reason for CFOs to take climate seriously comes from investors' appetite for green bonds—bonds that enable capital raising and investment for new and existing projects with environmental benefits. In 2019, new issuances on the green bond market reached around $250 billion overall, channeling more and more investments toward fighting climate change. Within this market, certified climate bonds, which are verified according to the type of physical asset or infrastructure they fund, allow companies to precisely align themselves with the 2015 Paris Agreement because they are consistent with its warming limit of 2 degrees Celsius. In addition to enabling the financing of environmental projects, these instruments may even represent an advantage in terms of cost of capital, since external financing can, in some cases, become indexed on ESG performance.

When Peter Bakker from the World Business Council for Sustainable Development said in 2012 that "accountants would save the planet," he was not far from the truth. Today, accountants are increasingly prioritizing climate change inside their organizations and beyond. Your CFO should be the next leader to follow.

A Better Way to Talk About the Climate Crisis

by Gretchen Gavett

Many of us care about the climate, but it can be challenging to talk about. It's easy to get bogged down in stats and statistics, for one. And it can be nerve-racking to approach someone if you don't already know what their beliefs on the topic are. (See "What Do People Really Believe About Climate Change?" hbr.org, January 27, 2020) Sometimes, it's easier to just keep our mouths shut.

Given the urgency of the climate crisis, however, many of us feel that silence is no longer an option. And Dr. Katharine Hayhoe, a climate scientist at Texas Tech University, is the person to talk to about how to talk about climate change. Hayhoe, whose 2018 TEDWomen talk on the subject has been viewed almost 2 million times, talks to everyone about the topic: Uber drivers, church ladies, Rotary Club members, business leaders, managers, elected officials, and more. People may have different backgrounds and views, but she's found a strategy that works: focusing on the heart—that is, what we collectively value—as opposed to the head.

So no matter your conversational goal, whether it's encouraging your company to act on climate issues or getting your employees to understand how the decisions they make affect your company's climate goals, this edited interview with Dr. Hayhoe is a great place to start.

HBR: *What should any leader take into consideration when talking to people—employees, clients, suppliers, etc.—about climate change?*

Hayhoe: Ultimately, whether you're training a new employee, reviewing best practices with a supplier, or just having a conversation about climate change with a client, follow this rule of thumb: Don't start with fear, judgment, condemnation, or guilt. And don't start with just overwhelming people with facts and figures. Do start by connecting the dots to what is already important to both of us, and then offer positive, beneficial, and practical solutions that we can engage in.

Why have you found that this method works best? And how does it lead people toward understanding the urgency of climate change and taking action?

Often we believe that to care about climate change we have to be a certain type of person: an environmentalist, someone who bikes to work, or is a vegan. And if we're not any of those things, then we think, "Why should climate change matter to me?" But the reality is that if we are a human living on planet Earth, then climate change already matters to every single one of us; we just haven't realized it yet. Why? Because climate change affects the economy, the availability of natural resources, prices, jobs, international competition, and more. Failing to account for climate change in future long-range planning could lose us a competitive edge even in a best-case scenario, and potentially mean the end of a product line or an entire business in the worst case. By connecting climate impacts to what we already care about, we can recognize the importance and urgency of taking action.

So if I'm a leader, what are some specific ways in which I can communicate with my employees that sustainability is a key part of their jobs?

I would start early. During their initial training, I would explain very clearly how our products, our production, and our waste contributes to the problem of climate change. If our production is very energy intensive or produces a lot of organic waste, for example, that means we may be generating massive amounts of greenhouse gases. If our goods are transported over long distances, that also requires fossil fuels that produce heat-trapping gases. And aside from the issue of climate change, if we produce a lot of non-recyclable waste that just piles up in landfills or the ocean, how much are we contributing to the pollution problem as well?

But I would also be sure to pair this information hand in hand with what we're doing to fix the problems from our end and how it's paying off. Give people analogies so it's really clear, so they can see it. I love giving examples of how many X worth of Y we've reduced; for example, something like "Through increasing the energy efficiency of our facilities, we have taken the equivalent of 500 cars off the road. Isn't that incredible? That's what we've been doing through our efforts." Or, "We have reduced our waste by 50%. That's the equivalent of X garbage trucks of waste per year." Or, "We are now powered by 38 wind turbines; that's X trainloads of coal we don't need to use anymore."

Finally—and this is the most important part!—I'd engage the employees themselves in the solutions. As humans, we want to be part of a solution. We want to make a difference. That is part of what gives us hope and what gives us energy, the idea that we're actually doing something good for the world.

So, for example, I might say, "We're aiming for an even better milestone. I want your ideas to help us get to this new milestone, too."

That's even more incentivizing, when you feel like a company encourages you and supports you and wants you to be part of their plan.

Does this advice extend to people who might not believe that climate change is that severe—or that it exists at all? What might this kind of conversation look like in a professional setting?

Only around 10% of the population is dismissive [of climate change], but they are a very loud 10%. Glance at the comment section of any online article on climate change, check out the responses to my tweets, or search for global warming videos on YouTube—they're everywhere. They're even at our Thanksgiving dinner, because just about every one of us has at least one person who is dismissive in the family. I do, too!

A person who is dismissive is someone who has built their identity on rejecting the reality of a changing climate because they believe the solutions represent a direct and immediate threat to all they hold dear. And in pursuit of that goal, they will reject anything: hundreds of scientific studies, thousands of experts, even the evidence of their own eyes. So, no, there is no point talking to a dismissive about climate science or impacts, unless you enjoy banging your head against the wall.

But it *can* be possible to have a constructive conversation with a dismissive—and I've had these!—by focusing solely on solutions that they don't see as a threat because they carry positive benefits and/or are good for their bottom line. And the fascinating thing is that once they are engaged in helping fix the problem, that very action can have the power to change a dismissive person's mind.

I want to end by asking about the importance of climate conversation over the next few years. I've heard anecdotally that companies are hearing more questions from younger job candidates or employees: "What are you doing? How are you addressing climate change as a company?" Does that resonate with you at all? Should companies be preparing for more conversations like these?

We see a very strong age gradient when it comes to levels of concern about climate change primarily among conservative populations, with younger people caring much more and being much more engaged than their elders. (Among more liberal populations, levels of concern are relatively high across all age groups.) At my own school, the number of students going to the president and asking, "What is our university doing?" has increased noticeably. I hear this anecdotally from colleagues all around the country, too. And when those students graduate, that's what they ask in their interviews, because they want to be part of the solution. Young people understand how urgent the problem is, and they know that there's no time to waste. A lot of them don't want to do a job that is not helping to fix this massive problem that we have.

If companies want to be competitive, if they want to hire the best and the brightest, the ones who are most engaged, the ones who are most in tune, the ones who really put their heart and their soul and their passion into their work, then they have to start talking about climate change differently. Because this is increasingly becoming something that young professionals really care about.

Originally published in January 2020. Reprint BG2001

The High Price of Efficiency

by Roger L. Martin

IN HIS LANDMARK 1776 work *The Wealth of Nations,* Adam Smith showed that a clever division of labor could make a commercial enterprise vastly more productive than if each worker took personal charge of constructing a finished product. Four decades later, in *On the Principles of Political Economy and Taxation,* David Ricardo took the argument further with his theory of comparative advantage, asserting that because it is more efficient for Portuguese workers to make wine and English workers to make cloth, each group would be better off focusing on its area of advantage and trading with the other.

These insights both reflected and drove the Industrial Revolution, which was as much about process innovations that reduced waste and increased productivity as it was about the application of new technologies. The notions that the way we organize work can influence productivity more than individual effort can and that specialization creates commercial advantage underlie the study of management to this day. In that sense Smith and Ricardo were the precursors of Frederick Winslow Taylor, who introduced the idea that management could be treated as a science—thus starting a movement that reached its apogee with W. Edwards Deming, whose Total Quality Management system was designed to eliminate all waste in the production process.

Smith, Ricardo, Taylor, and Deming together turned management into a science whose objective function was the elimination of waste—whether of time, materials, or capital. The belief in the unalloyed virtue of efficiency has never dimmed. It is embodied in multilateral organizations such as the World Trade Organization, aimed at making trade more efficient. It is ensconced in the Washington Consensus via trade and foreign direct-investment liberalization, efficient forms of taxation, deregulation, privatization, transparent capital markets, balanced budgets, and waste-fighting governments. And it is promoted in the classrooms of every business school on the planet.

Eliminating waste sounds like a reasonable goal. Why would we *not* want managers to strive for an ever-more-efficient use of resources? Yet as I will argue, an excessive focus on efficiency can produce startlingly negative effects, to the extent that superefficient businesses create the potential for social disorder. This happens because the rewards arising from efficiency get more and more unequal as that efficiency improves, creating a high degree of specialization and conferring an ever-growing market power on the most-efficient competitors. The resulting business environment is extremely risky, with high returns going to an increasingly limited number of companies and people—an outcome that is clearly unsustainable. The remedy, I believe, is for business, government, and education to focus more strongly on a less immediate source of competitive advantage: resilience. This may reduce the short-term gains from efficiency but will produce a more stable and equitable business environment in the long run. I conclude by describing what a resilience agenda might involve.

To understand why an unrelenting focus on efficiency is so dangerous, we must first explore our most basic assumptions about how the rewards from economic activities are distributed.

Outcomes Aren't Really Random

When predicting economic outcomes—incomes, profits, and so forth—we often assume that any payoffs at the individual level are random: dictated by chance. Of course, this is not actually so; payoffs are determined by a host of factors, including the choices we

Idea in Brief

The Problem

Management has come to be seen as a science whose purpose is to make commercial enterprises more efficient. But the single-minded pursuit of efficiency makes businesses less resilient.

Why It Happens

Businesses that are consistently more efficient earn an increasing share of available profits and can begin to game the market—and in time, industries become consolidated around a single dominant business model. This outcome carries a high risk of catastrophic failure and a high likelihood of exploitation.

The Solution

Business, government, and management education need to increase their emphasis on organizational resilience. This will involve limiting the size of businesses, introducing more friction into global trade and the capital markets, giving long-term investors a larger say in strategic decision making, creating jobs that are richer in learning opportunities, and offering educational programs that balance efficiency and resilience.

make. But those factors are so complex that as far as we can tell, economic outcomes might as well be determined by chance. Randomness is a simplifying assumption that fits what we observe.

If economic outcomes are random, statistics tells us that they will follow a Gaussian distribution: When plotted on a graph, the vast majority of payoffs will be close to the average, with fewer and fewer occurring the further we move in either direction. This is sometimes known as a normal distribution, because many things in our world follow the pattern, including human traits such as height, weight, and intelligence. It is also called a bell curve, for its shape. As data points are added, the whole becomes ever more normally distributed.

Because the Gaussian distribution is so prevalent in human life and in nature, we tend to expect it across domains. We believe that outcomes are and should be normally distributed—not just in the physical world but in the world writ large.

For example, we expect the distributions of personal incomes and firm performance within industries to be roughly Gaussian, and we build our systems and direct our actions accordingly. The classic way to think about an industry, however defined, is that it will have a small number of winners, a small number of losers (who are probably going out of business), and lots of competitors clustered in the middle. In such an environment, most efficiency gains are swiftly erased as others adopt them, and as firms fail, new ones replace them. This idealized form of competition is precisely what antitrust policy seeks to achieve. We don't want any single firm to grow so big and powerful that it shifts the distribution out of whack. And if the outcomes do follow a random distribution, and competitive advantage does not endure for long, competing on efficiency is sustainable.

But evidence doesn't justify the assumption of randomness in economic outcomes. In reality, efficiency gains create an enduring advantage for some players, and the outcomes follow an entirely different type of distribution—one named for the Italian economist Vilfredo Pareto, who observed more than a century ago that 20% of Italians owned 80% of the country's land. In a Pareto distribution, the vast majority of incidences are clustered at the low end, and the tail at the high end extends and extends. There is no meaningful mean or median; the distribution is not stable. Unlike what occurs in a Gaussian distribution, additional data points render a Pareto distribution even more extreme.

That happens because Pareto outcomes, in contrast to Gaussian ones, are not independent of one another. Consider height—a trait that, as mentioned, tracks a Gaussian distribution. One person's shortness does not contribute to another person's tallness, so height (within each sex) is normally distributed. Now think about what happens when someone is deciding whom to follow on Instagram. Typically, he or she looks at how many followers various users have. People with just a few don't even get into the consideration set. Conversely, famous people with lots of followers—for example, Kim Kardashian, who had 115 million at last count—are immediately attractive candidates *because* they already have lots of followers. The effect—many followers—becomes the cause of more of the effect: additional followers. Instagram followership, therefore, tracks a Pareto distribution: A very few people have the lion's share of followers, and a large proportion of people have only a few. The median number of followers is 150 to 200—a tiny fraction of what Kim Kardashian has.

The same applies to wealth. The amount of money in the world at any one moment is finite. Every dollar you have is a dollar that is not available to anyone else, and your earning a dollar is not independent of another person's earning a dollar. Moreover, the more dollars you have, the easier it is to earn more; as the saying goes, you need money to make money. As we're often told, the richest 1% of Americans own almost 40% of the country's wealth, while the bottom 90% own just 23%. The richest American is 100 billion times richer than the poorest American; by contrast, the tallest American adult is less than three times as tall as the shortest—demonstrating again how much wider the spread of outcomes is in a Pareto distribution.

We find a similar polarization in the geographic distribution of wealth. The rich are increasingly concentrated in a few places. In 1975, 21% of the richest 5% of Americans lived in the richest 10 cities. By 2012 the share had increased to 29%. The same holds for incomes. In 1966 the average per capita income in Cedar Rapids, Iowa, was equal to that in New York City; now it is 37% behind. In 1978 Detroit was on a par with New York City; now it is 38% behind. San Francisco was 50% above the national average in 1980; now it is 88% above. The comparable figures for New York City are 80% and 172%.

Business outcomes also seem to be shifting toward a Pareto distribution. Industry consolidation is increasingly common in the developing world: In more and more industries, profits are concentrated in a handful of companies. For instance, 75% of U.S. industries have become more concentrated in the past 20 years. In 1978 the 100 most profitable firms earned 48% of the profits of all publicly traded companies combined, but by 2015 the figure was an incredible 84%. (See the exhibit "The growing power of the few.") The success stories of the so-called new economy are in some measure responsible—the dynamics of platform businesses, where competitive advantages often derive from network effects, quickly convert Gaussian distributions to Pareto ones, as with Kim Kardashian and Instagram.

Let's examine how the quest for efficiency fits into this dynamic, along with the role of so-called monocultures and how power and self-interest lead some players to game the system, with corrosive results.

The Pressure to Consolidate

Complexity scholars, including UCLA's Bill McKelvey, have identified several factors that systematically push outcomes toward Pareto distributions. Among them are pressure on the system in question and ease of connection between its participants. Think about a sandpile—a favorite illustration of complexity theorists. You can add thousands of grains of sand one by one without triggering a collapse; each grain has virtually no effect. But then one additional grain starts a chain reaction in which the entire pile collapses; suddenly a single grain has a huge effect. If the sandpile were in a no-gravity context, however, it wouldn't collapse. It falls only as gravity pulls that final grain down, jarring the other grains out of position.

In business outcomes, gravity's equivalent is efficiency. Consider the U.S. waste-management industry. At one time there were thousands of little waste-management companies—garbage collectors—across the country. Each had one to several trucks serving customers on a particular route. The profitability of those thousands of companies was fairly normally distributed. Most clustered around the mean, with some highly efficient and bigger companies earning higher profits, and some weaker ones earning lower profits.

Then along came Wayne Huizenga, the founder of Waste Management (WM). Looking at the cost structure of the business, he saw that two big factors were truck acquisition (the vehicles were expensive, and because they were used intensively, they needed to be replaced regularly) and maintenance and repair (intensive use made this both critical and costly). Each small player bought trucks one or maybe a handful at a time and ran a repair depot to service its little fleet.

Huizenga realized that if he acquired a number of routes in a given region, two things would be possible. First, he would have much greater purchasing leverage with truck manufacturers and could acquire vehicles more cheaply. Second, he could close individual maintenance facilities and build a single, far more efficient one. As he proceeded, the effect—greater efficiency—became the cause of more of the effect. Huizenga generated the resources to keep buying small garbage companies and expanding into new territories, which made WM bigger and more efficient still. This put competitive pressure on all small operators, because WM could come into their territories and underbid them. Those smaller firms could either lose money or sell to WM. Huizenga's success represented a huge increase in pressure on the system.

Like a collapsing sandpile, the industry quickly consolidated, with WM as the dominant player, earning the highest profits; fellow consolidator Republic Services as the second-largest player, earning decent profits; several considerably smaller would-be consolidators earning few returns; and lots of tiny companies mainly operating at subsistence levels. The industry today is structured as a Pareto distribution, with WM as winner-take-most. The company earned more than $14 billion in 2017; Huizenga died (in March 2018) a multibillionaire.

If WM is so highly efficient, why should we object? Don't all consumers benefit, and does it matter whether WM or a collection of small firms issues sanitation workers' paychecks? The answer is that a superefficient dominant model elevates the risk of catastrophic failure. To understand why, we'll turn to an example from agriculture.

The Problem with Monocultures

Almonds were once grown in a number of places in America. But some locations proved better than others, and as in most production contexts, economies of scale could be had from consolidation. As it turns out, California's Central Valley is perfect for almond growing, and today more than 80% of the world's almonds are produced there. This is a classic business example of what biologists call a monoculture: A single factory produces a product, a single company holds sway in an industry, a single piece of software dominates all systems.

The growing power of the few

Since 1997 a strong majority of industries in the United States have become more concentrated. Many are now what economists consider "highly concentrated." This tends to correlate with low levels of competition, high consumer prices, and high profit margins.

Overall, concentration is increasing . . .

Plotting the change in concentration of more than 850 U.S. industries from 1997 to 2012 reveals upslopes in two-thirds of cases and downslopes in one-third. The large gap at the top of the downslope chart indicates that nearly all the industries that were highly concentrated in 1997 maintained or increased their concentration and that many industries are now very highly concentrated indeed.

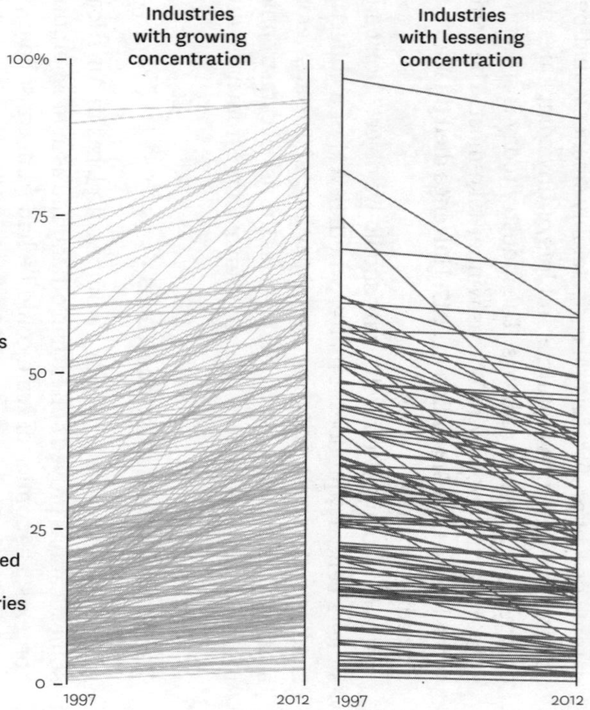

Industries with growing concentration

Industries with lessening concentration

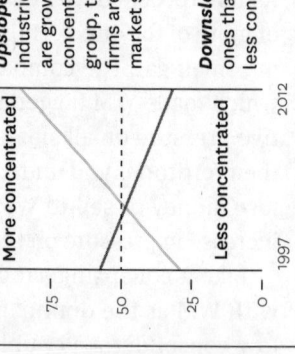

Key: How concentration is calculated

The portion of an industry that is controlled by the top four firms indicates that industry's concentration—a measure that changes over time.

More concentrated

Less concentrated

Upslopes show industries that are growing more concentrated: As a group, the top four firms are gaining market share.

Downslopes show ones that are growing less concentrated.

Source: U.S. Census Bureau, with analysis by the Economist (which provided this data to HBR)

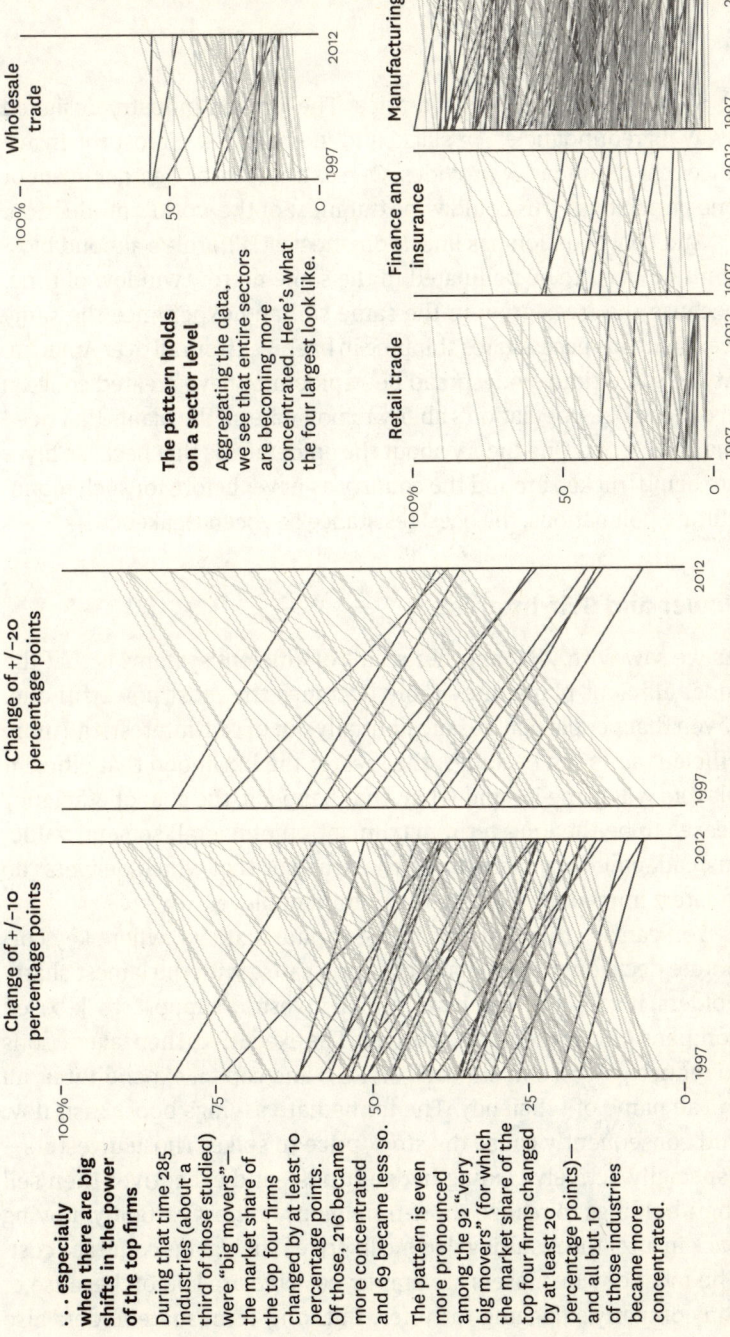

... especially when there are big shifts in the power of the top firms

During that time 285 industries (about a third of those studied) were "big movers" — the market share of the top four firms changed by at least 10 percentage points. Of those, 216 became more concentrated and 69 became less so.

The pattern is even more pronounced among the 92 "very big movers" (for which the market share of the top four firms changed by at least 20 percentage points)—and all but 10 of those industries became more concentrated.

Change of +/-10 percentage points

Change of +/-20 percentage points

The pattern holds on a sector level

Aggregating the data, we see that entire sectors are becoming more concentrated. Here's what the four largest look like.

Retail trade

Finance and insurance

Manufacturing

Wholesale trade

Note: When 2012 data was unavailable, data from the closest available year was used instead.

Such efficiency comes at a price. The almond industry designed away its redundancies, or slack, and in the process it lost the insurance that redundancy provides. One extreme local weather event or one pernicious virus could wipe out most of the world's production.

And consolidation has knock-on effects. California's almond blossoms all need to be pollinated in the same narrow window of time, because the trees grow in the same soil and experience the same weather. This necessitates shipping in beehives from all over America. At the same time, widespread bee epidemics have created concern about the U.S. population's ability to pollinate all the plants that need the bees' work. One theory about the epidemics is that because hives are being trucked around the country as never before for such monoculture pollinations, the bees' resistance has been weakened.

Power and Self-Interest

As we saw with WM, another result of efficient systems is that the most efficient player inevitably becomes the most powerful one. Given that people operate substantially out of self-interest, the more efficient a system becomes, the greater the likelihood that efficient players will game it—and when that happens, the goal of efficiency ceases to be the long-term maximization of overall societal value. Instead, efficiency starts to be construed as that which delivers the greatest immediate value to the dominant player.

You can see this dynamic in the capital markets, where key corporate decision makers make common cause with the largest shareholders. It goes like this: Institutional investors support stock-based compensation for senior executives. The executives then take actions to reduce payroll and cut back on R&D and capital expenditures, all in the name of efficiency. The immediate savings boost cash flow and consequently cause the stock price to spike. Those investors— especially actively trading hedge funds—and executives then sell their holdings to realize short-term gains, almost certainly moving back in after the resulting decline in price. Their gains come at a cost. The most obvious losers are employees who are laid off because of the company's flagging fortunes. But long-term shareholders also lose, because the company's future is imperiled. And customers suffer in terms of product quality, which is threatened as the company reduces its investment in making improvements.

Advocates of shareholder value argue that competition from entrants with superior products and services will compensate: The newcomers will employ the laid-off workers, customers will flock to their products, and shareholders will switch to the investments that promise better returns. But this assumes that the market is highly dynamic and that power is not concentrated among a handful of players. Those assumptions are valid in some sectors. The airline industry is one: The main assets—planes and gates—are relatively easy to acquire and dispose of, so whenever demand rises, new players can enter. But it is not easy to start a bank, build a chip factory, or launch a telecom company. (Ironically, entry is perhaps most difficult in some of the hottest areas of the new economy, where competitive advantage is often tied up with network effects that give incumbents a powerful boost.) And sometimes power becomes so concentrated that political action is needed to loosen the stranglehold of the dominant players, as in the antitrust movement of the 1890s.

The pension fund business provides a particularly egregious case of abuse by dominant insiders. In theory, fund managers should compete on the quality of their long-term investment decisions, because that is what delivers value to pensioners. But 19 of the 25 biggest U.S. pension funds, accounting for more than 50% of the assets of the country's 75 largest pension funds, are government-created and -regulated monopolies. Their customers have no choice of provider. If you are a teacher in Texas, the government mandates that the Teacher Retirement System of Texas—a government agency—manage your retirement assets. Fund managers' jobs, therefore, are relatively secure as long as they don't screw up in some obvious and public way. They are well placed to game the system.

The most straightforward way to do so is to accept inducements (typically offered by hedge funds) to invest in a particular way (one that benefits the hedge funds). In the past 10 years alone, senior executives of two of America's largest pension funds (government monopolies, I might add) were successfully prosecuted for taking multimillion-dollar bribes from hedge funds. We can assume that for each occurrence we see, many more escape our scrutiny—and the bribery isn't always so blatant, of course. Pension fund managers also accept luxurious trips they couldn't afford on their own, and many have left their positions for lucrative jobs at investment banks or hedge funds.

A particularly insidious pension-fund practice is lending stock to short-selling hedge funds (pension funds are the largest such lenders), in return for which the funds' managers earn relatively modest fees that help them meet their returns goals. The practice lets hedge funds create volatility in the capital markets, generating opportunities for traders but compromising the ability of company leaders to manage for the long term. Pensioners suffer while hedge funds and pension fund managers benefit.

The invisible hand of competition steers self-interested people to maximize value for all over the long term only in very dynamic markets in which outcomes really are random. And the process of competition itself works against this as long as it is focused exclusively on short-term efficiency, which, as we have seen, gives some players an advantage that often proves quite durable. As those players gain market share, they also gain market power, which makes it easier for them to gain value for their own interests by extracting rather than creating it.

How can society prevent the seemingly inevitable process of efficient entropy from taking hold? We must pay more attention to the less appreciated source of competitive advantage mentioned earlier: resilience.

Toward Resilience

Resilience is the ability to recover from difficulties—to spring back into shape after a shock. Think of the difference between being adapted to an existing environment (which is what efficiency delivers) and being adaptable to changes in the environment. Resilient systems are typically characterized by the very features—diversity and redundancy, or slack—that efficiency seeks to destroy.

To curb efficiency creep and foster resilience, organizations can:

Limit scale

In antitrust policy, the trend since the early 1980s has been to loosen enforcement so as not to impede efficiency. In fact, in the United States and the European Union, "increase in efficiency" is considered a legitimate defense of a merger challenged on the grounds that it would lead to excess concentration—even if the benefits of that efficiency gain would accrue to just a few powerful players.

We need to reverse that trend. Market domination is not an acceptable outcome, even if achieved through legitimate means such as organic growth. It isn't good for the world to have Facebook use its deep pockets from its core business to fund its Instagram subsidiary to destroy Snapchat. It isn't good to have Amazon kill all other retailers. It wasn't good to have Intel try to quash AMD decades ago by giving computer manufacturers discounts for not using AMD chips, and it wasn't good to have Qualcomm engage in similar behavior in recent years. Our antitrust policy needs to be much more rigorous to ensure dynamic competition, even if that means lower net efficiency.

Introduce friction

In our quest to make our systems more efficient, we have driven out all friction. It is as if we have tried to create a perfectly clean room, eradicating all the microbes therein. Things go well until a new microbe enters—wreaking havoc on the now-defenseless inhabitants.

To avoid such a trap, business and government need to engage in regular immunotherapy. Rather than design to keep all friction out of the system, we should inject productive friction at the right times and in the right places to build up the system's resilience.

For example, lower barriers to international trade should not be seen as an unalloyed good. Although David Ricardo clearly identified the efficiency gains from trade, he did not anticipate the impact on Pareto outcomes. Policy makers should deploy some trade barriers to ensure that a few massive firms don't dominate national markets, even if such domination appears to produce maximum efficiency. Small French baguette bakers are protected from serious competition by a staggering array of regulations. The result: Although not cheap, French baguettes are arguably the best in the world. Japan's nontariff barriers make it nearly impossible for foreign car manufacturers to penetrate the market, but that hasn't stopped Japan from giving rise to some of the most successful global car companies.

Friction is also needed in the capital markets. The current goal of U.S. regulators is to maximize liquidity and reduce transaction costs. This has meant that they first allowed the New York Stock Exchange to acquire numerous other exchanges and then allowed the NYSE itself to be acquired by the Intercontinental Exchange. A fuller realization of this goal would increase the pace at which the billionaire hedge-fund owners already at the far end of the Pareto distribution of wealth trade in fewer but ever bigger markets and generate even-more-extreme Pareto outcomes. U.S. regulators should act more like the EU, which blocked the merger of Europe's two biggest players, the London Stock Exchange and the Deutsche Börse. And they should stop placing obstacles in the way of new players seeking to establish new exchanges, because those obstacles only solidify the power of consolidated players. In addition, short selling and the volatility it engenders could be dramatically reduced if the government prohibited public sector pension funds (such as the California Public Employees' Retirement System and the New York State Common Retirement Fund) from lending stock.

Promote patient capital

Common equity is supposed to be a long-term stake: Once it is given, the company notionally has the capital forever. In practice, however, anybody can buy that equity on a stock market without the company's permission, which means that it can be a short-term investment. But long-term capital is far more helpful to a company trying to create and deploy a long-term strategy than short-term capital is. If you give me $100 but say that you can change how it is to be used with 24 hours' notice, that money isn't nearly as valuable to me as if you said I can use it as I want for 10 years. If Warren Buffett's desired holding period for stock is, as he jokes, "forever," while the quantitative arbitrage hedge fund Renaissance Technologies holds investments only for milliseconds, Buffett's capital is more valuable than that of Renaissance.

The difference in value to the company notwithstanding, the two types of equity investments are given exactly the same rights. That's a mistake; we should base voting rights on the period for which capital is held. Under that approach, each common share would give its holder one vote per day of ownership up to 3,650 days, or 10 years. If you held 100 shares for 10 years, you could vote 365,000 shares. If you sold those shares, the buyer would get 100 votes on the day of purchase. If the buyer became a long-term holder, eventually that would rise to 365,000 votes. But if the buyer were an activist hedge fund like Pershing Square, whose holding period is measured in months, the interests of long-term investors would swamp its influence on strategy, quite appropriately. Allocating voting rights in this way would reward long-term shareholders for providing the most valuable kind of capital. And it would make it extremely hard for activist hedge funds to take effective control of companies, because the instant they acquired a share, its rights would be reduced to a single vote.

Some argue that this would entrench bad management. It would not. Currently, investors who are unhappy with management can sell their economic ownership of a share along with one voting right. Under the proposed system, unhappy investors could still sell their economic ownership of a share along with one voting right. But if a lot of shareholders were happy with management and yet an activist wanted to make a quick buck by forcing the company to sell assets, cut R&D investment, or take other actions that could harm its future, that activist would have a reduced ability to collect the voting rights to push that agenda.

Create good jobs
In our pursuit of efficiency, we have come to believe that routine labor is an expense to be minimized. Companies underinvest in training and skill development, use temporary and part-time

workers, tightly schedule to avoid "excess hours," and design jobs to require few skills so that they can be exceedingly low paid. This ignores the fact that labor is not just a cost; it is a resource that can be productive—and the current way of managing it drives down that productivity as it reduces the dollar cost.

What if we focused on longer-term productivity? Instead of designing jobs for low-skill, minimum-wage clock punchers, what if we designed them to be productive and valuable? In *The Good Jobs Strategy,* MIT's Zeynep Ton describes how some discount retailers have doubled down on their employees, seeking more-engaged and more-knowledgeable workers, better customer service, lower turnover, and increased sales and profits, all leading to further investment. A key but counterintuitive element of the strategy is to build in slack so that employees have time to serve customers in unanticipated yet valuable ways.

It's not just businesses that can benefit from a good jobs strategy. The cheap labor model is extremely costly to the wider economy. When they cut labor costs, companies such as Walmart simply transfer expenses traditionally borne by employers to taxpayers. A recent congressional study evaluated the impact of a single 200-person Walmart store on the federal budget. It turns out that each employee costs taxpayers $2,759 annually (in 2018 dollars) for benefits necessitated by the low wages, such as food and energy subsidies, housing and health care assistance, and federal tax credits. With 11,000 stores and 2.3 million employees, the company's much-touted labor efficiency carries a hefty price tag indeed.

Teach for resilience

Management education focuses on the single-minded pursuit of efficiency—and trains students in analytic techniques that deploy short-term proxies for measuring that quality. As a result, graduates head into the world to build (inadvertently, I believe) highly efficient businesses that largely lack resilience.

Management deans, professors, and students would undoubtedly beg to differ. But the curricula show otherwise. Finance teaches the pursuit of efficient financial structures. Efficient cost management is the goal of management accounting. Human resources teaches efficient staffing. Marketing is about the efficient targeting of and selling to segments. Operations management is about increasing plants' efficiency. The overarching goal is the maximization of shareholder value.

Of course, none of these in itself is a bad thing. A corporation *should* maximize shareholder value—in the very long term. The problem is that today's market capitalization is what defines shareholder value. Similarly, this quarter's reductions in labor costs are what define efficiency. And the optimal capital structure for this year's operating environment is what defines an efficient deployment of capital. Those are all short-term ways of assessing long-term outputs.

If we continue to promote these short-term proxies, managers will seek to maximize them, despite the cost to long-term resilience. And activist hedge funds will take control of companies and cause them to act in ways that appear, if judged by short-term proxies, to be highly efficient. Those funds will be applauded by regulators and institutional proxy voting advisers, all of whom will continue to think their actions have nothing to do with the production of more-fragile companies.

For the sake of the future of democratic capitalism, management education must become a voice for, not against, resilience.

In his 1992 work *The End of History and the Last Man,* Francis Fukuyama argued that the central theme of modern history is the struggle between despotism and what we now know as democratic capitalism. The latter certainly has the upper hand. But it's a stretch to claim, as Fukuyama did, that it has won the war. Every day we find evidence that economic efficiency, which has traditionally underpinned democratic capitalism, is failing to distribute the concomitant gains. The stark realities of the Pareto distribution threaten the electorate's core belief that the combination of democracy and capitalism can make the lives of a majority of us better over time. Our system is much more vulnerable and much less fair than we like to think. That needs to change.

Success breeds inequality: What the data shows by Jacob Greenspon and Darren Karn.

The recovery from the Great Depression of the 1930s was characterized by a degree of social solidarity and a narrowing of the gap between rich and poor. The recovery from the Great Recession of 2007–2009 has been very different. In the United States, for example, the gap between the wage growth of the rich and that of the poor has widened significantly, while the difference in earnings between the most successful firms and the rest has grown dramatically.

Rich people are getting (a lot) richer

Since 1971 incomes for the bottom half of the wealth distribution have been stagnant, and they have grown by only a third for Americans in the 50th to 90th percentiles—but they have more than doubled for the top 10%.

Income growth (1971=1)

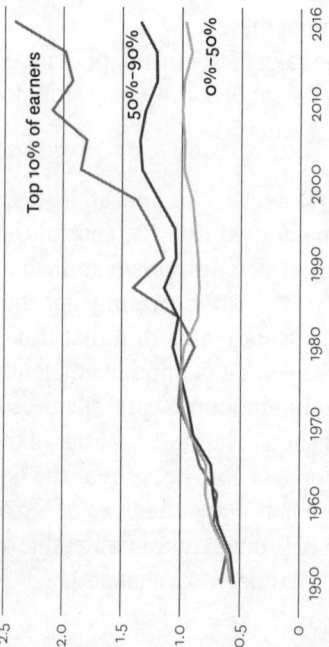

Source: "Income and Wealth Inequality in America, 1949–2016," by Moritz Kuhn, Moritz Schularick, and Ulrike I. Steins (working paper)

The wealthiest firms are pulling away

The gap between top-earning and median firms in the United States has grown drastically since 1990. The latest data shows that firms at or above the 90th percentile of earnings have returns that nearly double their capital investments, compared with returns of just 15% for median firms.

Return on invested capital

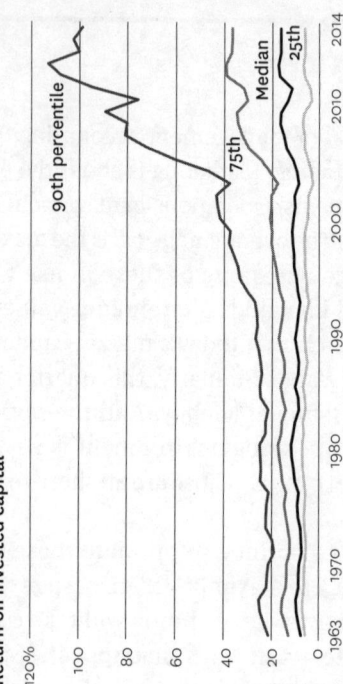

Source: "A Firm-Level Perspective on the Role of Rents in the Rise in Inequality," by Jason Furman and Peter Orszag (Obama White House Archives)

Stocks have fully recovered—but housing prices have not

The weak recovery of housing prices after the 2008 crash has meant that Americans whose wealth is based in housing assets have become poorer. The bottom 50% of Americans lost 16% of their wealth, on average, from 2007 to 2016 (after adjusting for inflation). But the main stock-market indices were 30% above their 2007 levels by 2016—a rebound that largely benefited the wealthy.

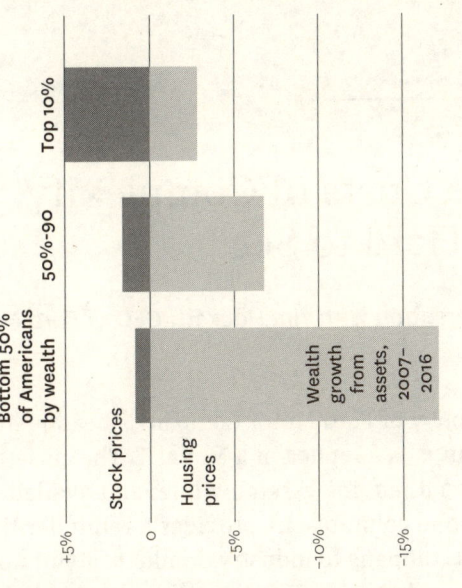

Source: "Income and Wealth Inequality in America, 1949–2016," by Moritz Kuhn, Moritz Schularick, and Ulrike I. Steins (working paper)

The tax system has grown less progressive

Federal income-tax rates for most Americans increased steadily throughout the 1970s before falling sharply after the 1981 and 1986 Reagan tax cuts. Taxes paid by the highest-earning Americans on their final dollars of income have dropped sharply since 1966, while taxes paid by those near the middle of the income distribution have declined by far less—and in some cases have increased.

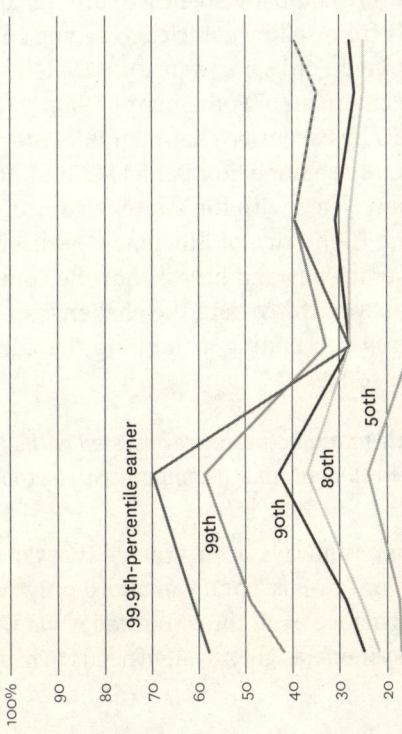

Source: Data from the World Inequality Database, the National Bureau of Economic Research, and the Tax Foundation; analysis by the Martin Prosperity Institute

"The Costs of Complexity Are Hard to See"

A conversation with Jim Hackett, CEO of Ford Motor Company

In the lobby of Ford Motor Company's headquarters, in Dearborn, Michigan, sits a replica of a Model T. The car—the first to be produced on a moving assembly line, and available for many years in only one color, black—provides a reminder that efficiency can propel a company to industry dominance. But upstairs on the 12th floor, president and CEO Jim Hackett is leading the firm toward a different goal: what he calls *corporate fitness*. Hackett, who led the office furniture company Steelcase through an IPO and championed its shift from selling cubicles to selling collaborative open workspaces, joined Ford's board in 2013. He left that post in 2016 to become the chairman of Ford Smart Mobility. In May of 2017 he was named CEO by executive chairman Bill Ford. In a recent conversation with HBR senior editor Daniel McGinn, Hackett—who has worked for many years with the strategy adviser Roger L. Martin (author of "The High Price of Efficiency")—discussed the difference between efficiency and fitness, how he communicates complex ideas to his workforce, and the challenge of convincing Wall Street that he is succeeding at moving the company forward. Edited excerpts follow.

HBR: *Automobile manufacturers are obsessed with efficiency. Isn't Roger Martin's argument, that a company can be too efficient, sort of heretical?*

Hackett: There's always been a meme that goes: "Do you want speed, quality, or low cost? You can afford only two of the three." Efficiency is a balance of all three. But today we win or lose on the basis of better system design. A system needs to have efficiency built in, because if it uses too many resources, it can't survive. But winning isn't just about efficiency.

Is it about what you've termed "corporate fitness"? What do you mean by that?

People ask, "Why don't you just say, 'Let's reduce costs'?" But when I say "fitness," I'm thinking about what Darwin learned about survival of the fittest—that a species evolves to be more competitive. Being competitive now is about a lot of factors. How long does it take an order to be delivered? How many products does a company offer? Do you have the right or the wrong people? Businesses win by having a combination of the right people and the right design.

Your ideas about how organizations evolve stem from Darwin?

Yes. Years ago a professor gave me a bunch of white papers written by physicists at the Santa Fe Institute, and I became voraciously interested in them. I began to learn about complex systems theory, which holds that evolution isn't just a biological process; it can apply to social organizations as well. I found myself asking, "If Darwin's ideas exist in nature, who am I to say they don't apply in business? What if they apply everywhere?"

How did you apply them at Steelcase?

I was the CEO at Steelcase for 20 years, so like Darwin with biology, I got to see the company evolve over time. I found myself in a wave pattern, where I was shrinking the company during recessions, then growing it, then shrinking it, then growing it. That's not healthy. We needed to design the company for all states, by lowering our average costs. That's part of what I mean by fitness.

It sounds as though you define fitness as the ability to deal with a shifting landscape. So if a marathoner is good at long races, that's efficient, but a decathlete can tackle a variety of events, so he or she is fitter. Is that it?

That's close. Let me use a different analogy. Imagine you and I are racing up a big mountain. I beat you, but only by a nanosecond.

Imagine I show up the next year for the race and say to myself, "I've got to do better than I did last year." I start off the race, and I'm winning—my time is better. But the environment on the mountain has changed, so I need to perform much better than last year to win again. That's what makes this hard—it's dynamic. That's the Darwinian part. Businesses typically look at market share, profits, and earnings per share. Those are important things. But it isn't just our earnings per share versus those of other auto manufacturers that count. It's our cycle time versus Amazon's, for example. Amazon doesn't make cars, but it could sell them, or it could sell auto parts. That's what happens with disruption. You probably don't lose to the standard competitors; it's the mutation coming at you that matters. You can't count on the mountain you're climbing to stay the same.

Your efforts to make Ford fitter include building your models on fewer platforms and reducing the number of options and configurations consumers can choose from. Ford made a big push in that direction during the 1990s. Why didn't it work?

Complexity creeps in over time. In nature, forest fires actually help forests thrive, by burning away the underbrush. At Ford we're right in the middle of that work of eliminating complexity. We're getting really great results. My concern is that the gestation period in the auto industry is longer than in the industry I came from. I don't want people to lose confidence; I know these theories work. People say, "We haven't seen it yet." They will. The costs of complexity are hard to see until they're gone.

You have an affinity for very complex ideas, and you describe them in complicated ways. As a leader, does that create challenges?

Unquestionably. The good news is, I've been through this before, at Steelcase. My job is to help paint a picture people can understand. I'm purposely using different language. Why say "fitness" instead of "reduce costs"? Because the solution to reducing costs is to hold your breath. And when you hold your breath but don't change anything else, the costs come back. During the Great Recession, Ford brought its breakeven down significantly. But the costs all came back, because the company didn't change the design.

I'm working on the communication part. One way is by delegating some of it. Another is by boiling down our plan so that people can follow it.

Back in 2012 or 2013, near the end of Alan Mulally's time as CEO, what could have been done differently to put Ford in a better position today?

I always start by saying the management team in place was really smart. So what did it miss? In my assessment, it missed that our competitors were all bankrupt when our strategy emerged. Ford was the stronger, fitter player, which allowed it to avoid bankruptcy—and on one level, that was an advantage. The negative was that competitors came out of bankruptcy stronger and fitter. Bankruptcy forced them to redesign their businesses. What Ford missed was that competitors were getting fitter while we were on a trajectory we could celebrate, so we didn't change enough.

Does Ford's status as a family-controlled company make it easier to pursue large-scale change?

The Fords are what we call long-arc shareholders. They have been owners since 1903, and they retain 40% of the general voting power. That tells you they've got a deep commitment. Bill Ford wants to win. He's proud of Ford's forward-leaning attributes—the way the company treats its people, the way it affects the environment. But his eyes get really big when he drives a Mustang; the vitality of the product matters deeply to him. We had long talks before I took this job. I told him he had a bunch of people he could choose from and that I might not be the best guy. I wasn't selling myself, because I was being asked to consider the job.

Why might you not have been "the best guy"?

It relates to something you asked about earlier: communication. Was the nature of the transformation going to be really simple and well understood in the early periods? I told him it would take a while for the internal organization to get traction. We're going to get results, and then Wall Street will follow.

Since becoming CEO, you've announced that Ford will stop selling most models of cars in the United States. How did you conclude you can't play to win in that segment?

If you drew an outline around the Model T, you'd have a silhouette. I ask people, "Where is that silhouette today? Is it still on the market?" No. Over time that silhouette—the shape of the car—has changed, because the world, the markets, and the size of people have changed.

Sedans mutated because buyer preference turned to larger silhouettes, such as sport utility vehicles. In the past, automakers were reluctant to stop selling small cars, because they were afraid that if fuel prices went up, they'd get nailed. Low fuel prices teach us what people really prefer: They prefer larger silhouettes. But now we have new forms of propulsion—battery electrics and hybrids. We're designing vehicles that will deliver a larger silhouette without a penalty in fuel efficiency.

Roger Martin argues that efficiency increases risk by reducing redundancy and resiliency. Is Ford less resilient because of its reliance on the F-150 pickup truck, which is responsible for all the company's profits?

We're actually in a really favored place with the F-150, where we play to win. We can take more risks with it. We have other silhouettes with properties of the F-150 that we get to exploit. The Super Duty— a pickup with more horsepower and higher torque—grew faster than the F-150 this year. In meetings we talk about what makes the pickup truck so fit today. Why is it so popular? It's because buyers have jobs that have to be done that the F-150 is very good at. So we ask: Do we really understand its performance? And how can we support those jobs even better in the future?

Ford, like other carmakers, is investing a lot in autonomous vehicles. When will they hit the market?

My optimism about that future is really high. It's probably just further out than people realize. There's a quote that goes something like this: People overestimate the impact of technology in the short run and underestimate its impact in the long run. That's probably true in this area. When those vehicles do arrive, they'll be a dramatic disrupter.

Is corporate fitness especially important for a global manufacturer during an era of political uncertainty and shifts in trade policy?

Trade systems are best for us when they're in equilibrium. You can design your business around equilibrium. We don't want to be in a trade war; that's a bad idea. We don't need certainty—we can deal with the ups and downs of weather or raw materials shortages. But it's hard to prepare for a sudden decision to put a 25% tax on something.

You use the word "teach" more than most other CEOs do. Is that an important part of the way you lead?

In a job like this, you have high-powered people working for you. They don't need you to wind them up every day. So the role I have to play is, rather than tell them what to do, help them see how wisdom and curiosity can help us design better. I've asked employees to let me play that role and to have patience with it. We're getting into a rhythm together.

In your industry there's a lot of focus on Tesla, which built a product people love but has struggled to scale up production. What do you make of its challenges?

People sometimes say something isn't rocket science. I actually have a competitor, Elon Musk, who is a rocket scientist. I have tremendous respect for him because of the way he questions the design of the system.

Ford builds a vehicle every four seconds. So there's something about the fitness of our system that those who are starting out can't yet equal. How it all gets choreographed is a really hard physics problem—just as hard as putting a rocket into space. But there's no question the fitness of the system has improved because of Tesla's arrival. Customers now expect over-the-air updates of automobile software [because Tesla provides them]. That will be a table stakes thing in the car business that can be attributed to Musk.

Does Tesla's presence help you convince employees that they need to look beyond GM and Toyota and imagine new kinds of competitors?

When a car company gets 400,000 or 500,000 preorders for a vehicle, you have to pay attention. The humility here is what Darwin taught us: There's no guarantee for your future. That doesn't mean we can't be optimistic. It just means the design probably won't stay the same.

Originally published in January–February 2019. Reprint R1901B

Reigniting Growth

by Chris Zook and James Allen

MOST SUCCESSFUL COMPANIES EVENTUALLY FACE a predictable crisis that we call *stall-out*—a sudden large drop in revenue and profit growth or a collapse of once high shareholder returns to well below the cost of capital. Stall-out occurs when the growth engine that powered a company to success stops working. This rarely happens because the business model has suddenly become obsolete—a common misconception. Rather, our research shows that the business has almost always become too complex, most often owing to bureaucracy that slows the company's metabolism, or internal dysfunction that distorts information and hampers managers' ability to make rapid decisions and take swift action on them. When we talk to executives about the symptoms of stall-out, their words vary, but the reasons remain the same. *We've lost touch with customers. We're drowning in process and PowerPoint. We have no shortage of opportunities, but somehow we can no longer act decisively. What was once such a high-energy ride now feels like trying to pilot a plane with no thrust and unresponsive controls.*

In an analysis of 8,000 global companies, we found that two-thirds of those successful enough to reach $500 million in revenue faced stall-out over the 15 years ending in 2013—including notables such as Panasonic, Time Warner, Carrefour, Bristol-Myers Squibb, Alcatel-Lucent, Philips, Sony, and Mazda. More alarming still, for 50 large companies in prolonged stall-out, we found that the onset had usually been sudden: Momentum fell sharply over just a year or two, with growth rates dropping from double digits to low single digits or even negative numbers—a finding consistent with past research (see "When Growth Stalls," HBR, March 2008).

To be sure, external forces put pressure on incumbent companies. Strategy—the external chessboard of business—still matters. Yet competitive strategies are more similar than they used to be, more easily copied, and of shorter duration. The roots of success or failure increasingly lie in the ability of companies to remain fast, perceptive, innovative, and adaptable. Internally thriving companies can respond to shifts in their competitive environments, identifying—and executing—strategies that sustain their dominance. When we polled 377 business leaders, 94% of those in companies with revenue of more than $5 billion told us that internal dysfunction—not lack of opportunity or unmatchable competitor capabilities—was now the main barrier to their continued profitable growth.

Yes, stall-out may be predictable, but it can be overcome. We argue in a forthcoming book that most companies with sustainable growth share attitudes and behaviors: (1) They view themselves as business insurgents, fighting in behalf of underserved customers; (2) they have an obsession with the front line, where the business meets the customer; and (3) they foster a mindset that includes a deep sense of responsibility for how resources are used and for long-term results. Because these qualities are most vibrant in companies led by bold, ambitious founders, we call them "the founder's mentality." Since 2000, returns to shareholders in large public companies where the founder is still involved have been three times those for other companies. But any leadership team can harness the revitalizing effects of the founder's mentality. In some cases, a once dominant mindset has been lost over time and may need to be rebuilt from a few vestiges. But these three qualities can help any company restart its growth engine by removing gunk and complexity that has built up over the years, inhibiting the clean execution of strategy.

1. Rediscover Your Insurgent Mission

When stall-out occurs, it is almost always connected to creeping complexity. "No single bad decision or tactic or person was to blame," Howard Schultz said after returning to the CEO position at Starbucks in 2008 amid shrinking revenue, collapsing margins, and

Idea in Brief

The Problem

Growing companies often face the predictable crisis of stall-out—a sudden large drop in revenue and profit growth. The culprits are usually complexity and bureaucracy.

The Solution

Leaders need to rediscover the "founder's mentality"—attitudes and behaviors that are strongly associated with founding management teams and can revitalize the business.

The Principles

Stalling companies should drastically reduce complexity and excess cost, refresh the mission, and configure the organization to focus obsessively on the business's front line. Finally, they should instill an owner's mindset that eschews bureaucracy and celebrates speed and accountability.

a decline in stock price of more than 75%. Starbucks's stall-out was sudden and dramatic, he acknowledged, but it resulted from damage that had been "slow and quiet, incremental, like a single loose thread that unravels a sweater inch by inch."

To begin tackling stall-out, companies need to strip away complexity and excess cost in order to liberate resources, narrow focus, and harness the vigor that drove the company's early growth. We studied 10 successful rescue-and-rebirth operations and found that all of them involved reducing operating costs by at least 8% and sometimes more than 25%.

Successful attacks on complexity are led from the top down and proceed in a sequence. First the company must shed noncore assets and businesses. Next it must develop a simpler strategy for the remaining businesses. Then it can attack complexity in the core processes. Finally, it can focus on reducing product complexity in design, variations, and customization. We've seen leadership teams attempt transformation in the reverse order, only to become trapped in details and wear down the organization before getting to what really makes most transformations successful: reducing high-level complexity and cost.

We have found that as companies grow in size, internal budget processes become democratic, spreading resources evenly across businesses and opportunities. But democratic investment in the face of crisis is a sure path to mediocrity. The opposite is needed to reverse stall-out. At companies where it was avoided, leaders had made bold investment decisions to redifferentiate the company, usually establishing a major new capability that set off waves of growth.

Once back in shape, companies must renew their view of themselves as business insurgents. This does not require promoting a martial culture or abusing the metaphor of "waging war" on competitors. Rather, companies should view their customers as underserved and their industries as setting insufficient standards, and should constantly emphasize what is special about themselves. Bold goals—not just the aim of living to fight another day—will sustain growth. As they become very large, organizations may find maintaining an insurgent mission hard, but it's not impossible. Google's mission to "organize the world's information," for example, is at once specific to Google and nearly infinite in its ambition.

A company should even be prepared to shrink significantly if that's what is needed to regroup, redeploy, and restart profitable growth. Consider the case of Perpetual, the oldest trust company in Australia, which recovered from stall-out by reducing its operating costs by 20%, stripping away noncore businesses, and rejuvenating around its founder's original mission.

Established in 1886 to manage trusts and estates for Australia's scions, Perpetual led the market for most of its history. But as it grew, it diversified into 11 new business areas, and by 2011 the company was struggling. Its share price had fallen from a high of $84 to $24 in only four years. Profits were down by nearly 70%, with no bottom in sight. Shareholders were calling publicly for a major overhaul, and the company had hired its third CEO in 12 months, Geoff Lloyd.

When he arrived, he "found an organization that was internally competitive and externally cooperative," Lloyd told us. "We had grown incredibly complex over time by entering more businesses, and we were not the leader in most of them." Lloyd concluded that to save Perpetual, he would have to return the company to its core mission: the protection of Australia's wealth. That, he realized, meant making the company "faster, more confident, and, above all, simpler."

Lloyd began by replacing 10 of the 11 members of the management team with people who had no vested interest in past decisions. With his new staff in place, he launched Transformation 2015, five initiatives designed to bring about swift complexity reduction at all levels. One was the "portfolio" initiative, which reduced the number of businesses from 11 to three (just two businesses were responsible for about 95% of profits), cut real estate holdings by half, and eliminated more than 100 legacy funding structures. Another, the "operating model" initiative, reduced the staff at headquarters by more than 50%. Lloyd and his team found that back-office support, staff functions, and redundant controls accounted for 60% of total costs. In other words, the company was putting only 40% of its money toward sales, customer service, and investment—its core activities. Furthermore, it was relying on more than 3,000 computer systems and applications.

Cutting back—on businesses, staff, computer systems, and more—was central to the transformation plan. But Lloyd and his team also crafted a plan to gain market share by investing in the company's core. He convened town hall meetings, which had never before been held at Perpetual, to discuss the company's situation and its future and to reignite enthusiasm for its core values. "We labored over the wording of our mission and strategy," Lloyd told us, explaining that he felt it was essential for employees to refocus on the founding principles of the company. In the process, he learned a remarkable thing: Perpetual's original trust business was so strong that it still had its first customer—125 years later.

His strategies brought about a stunning turnaround. Perpetual's stock price has more than doubled since Lloyd took over; employee engagement has measurably increased; the company is gaining share in its core markets; and net profits have tripled.

2. Obsess Over Your Business's Front Line

Companies that sustain growth live and breathe the front line of their business. This obsession, which can often be traced back to a strong founder, shows up in three ways: an elevated status for frontline employees, a preoccupation with individual customers at all levels of the company, and an institutional curiosity about the details of the business. A frontline obsession is most obvious in "high-touch" consumer businesses such as luxury hospitality. But the trait can exist in subtler ways in a range of industries: Consider the product obsession of Steve Jobs and the legendary attention to detail of the wine pioneer Robert Mondavi, who believed in the saying "The best fertilizer for a vineyard is the owner's footsteps."

The Home Depot, the largest home-improvement retailer in the world, provides an example of how losing a frontline obsession can lead to stall-out—and how renewing it can reignite growth. The company's initial success could be traced to its remarkable founders, Bernard Marcus and Arthur Blank, who devoted themselves to building a close advisory relationship with customers. Their corporate mantra was "Whatever it takes." The founders even trained store employees in customer service themselves. Employees, in turn, offered clinics on home improvement projects for customers and were always available in stores to provide knowledgeable advice. The strategy set the company apart and generated powerful customer loyalty, and for years The Home Depot was a major success story. From its founding, in 1978, until 2000, it consistently eclipsed its 20% annual earnings growth targets. But in December 2000, after missing an earnings target and having become increasingly concerned about antiquated systems—especially IT—in a company that was approaching $50 billion in revenue, the board of directors hired Robert Nardelli, a senior executive from GE, to introduce some big-company discipline as CEO.

Nardelli created a command-and-control environment. By early 2006, 98% of the company's top 170 executives were new to their jobs, and 56% of the new managers at headquarters had come from the outside. Fresh leadership, especially in the area of systems, was probably needed, but this changing of the guard failed to build on the deep strengths that had once made the company special and beloved by its customers. Nardelli and his team neglected customer relationships and frontline enthusiasm in favor of boosting quarterly profits. Many long-serving full-time employees were replaced by lower-paid part-time workers, and customer service collapsed. "Do it yourself," some people joked, was now "Find it yourself." When the University of Michigan released its 2006 American Customer Satisfaction Index, The Home Depot had slipped to last among major U.S. retailers. The board held meetings in the field and found a consistent pattern: concern for the future, disempowerment of long-time store employees, and a feeling that the social contract between the company, its employees, and its customers was being breached.

Greg Brenneman, the longest-serving board member and a global turnaround expert, told us, "You could see the serious trouble bubbling up under the surface. Store managers were feeling shackled by dozens of financial templates and metrics that took time away from customers and running the stores. The most experienced store employees, the real experts on plumbing or electricity, had been let go and replaced with less experienced and cheaper part-time store workers. Foot traffic, the lifeblood of any retailer, was dropping. New stores were not generating good returns, leading to further staff cuts. We were stalling out and needed to change course."

The deterioration of the customer experience was at the root of the company's woes, and thus it illuminated a path back to sustainable growth. In 2007 the board replaced Nardelli with Frank Blake. On his very first day on the job, Blake spoke to all employees using The Home Depot's internal television station and quoted extensively from Marcus and Blank's book, *Built from Scratch*. In particular, he highlighted two of their charts. One listed their core values, and the other gave pride of place, at the top of an inverted triangle, to the company's front line: its stores, where customers and employees interact.

Many of Blake's first initiatives focused on restoring the "orange-apron cult": knowledgeable store employees, easily identifiable by their aprons, who focused on high levels of customer service. Taking advice from Marcus, Blake also began anonymously visiting stores on "undercover missions," as he called them. These proved so valuable that he instructed his senior executives to adopt a "management by walking about" approach, something most had never done before.

Like Lloyd at Perpetual, Blake then set out to reduce complexity, restructuring the businesses and closing money-losing stores—essentially, shrinking to grow. He also increased the employee bonus pool by a factor of seven, rehired some veterans, and asked store managers to return to the pre-Nardelli policy of giving out honor badges to employees who had been exceptionally attentive to customers.

Eight years ago The Home Depot had stalled out and was facing the prospect of free fall. But as of the end of 2015, thanks to Blake's renewal of the founders' mentality, the company has reenergized its employees and repersonalized its customer experience—a return to core principles that has driven the company's stock from about $25 a share in 2009 to more than $130 by December 2015.

3. Instill an Owner's Mindset

The third factor in reversing stall-out involves a management idea that first came into vogue 40 years ago: the owner's mindset. Designed to instill balance-sheet discipline and accountability by aligning employees and shareholders, this concept is frequently misunderstood. Too often, it implies an incumbent's mindset: a concern with hunkering down and extracting value from the existing business, and a loss of interest in innovating, serving customers uniquely, and fully valuing frontline employees.

At its best, the owner's mindset focuses on the long term, has a strong bias toward speed and action, and embraces personal responsibility for employees' actions and for how resources are used. The power of the owner's mindset is central to the rise of the private equity industry—a reaction against the bureaucracy, poor cost management, and complexity that beset many large companies. When we analyzed the returns of deals within several private equity funds, we found that businesses sold by large public companies in which management had seemingly lost the incentives of ownership subsequently earned nearly 50% more than the others. After private equity firms had restored the owner's mindset, these companies benefited from increased speed, reduced bureaucracy, a more

How to Get Started

HERE ARE SOME WAYS to prepare your team to reignite growth.

Create a "founder's mentality" scorecard

Manage it as a strategic asset. Does your mission keep you fighting in behalf of your customers? Does your company focus on the front line of the business? Do employees embrace an owner's mindset that eschews bureaucracy, is focused on speed, and demands personal accountability?

Benchmark against your most successful upstart competitors

Are they winning on speed and cost? Commit as a leadership team to closing the gap.

Launch a campaign against bureaucracy

Look for management layers and processes that have outlived their usefulness. Eliminate them.

Get the leadership team out of the office

The front line is where the answer to a growth stall-out is most likely to reside.

Reexamine the precepts and practices of your founders or early leaders

When was the company at its best? What has been lost along the way that needs to be restored?

Look outside for help inside

You might reach out to retired founders or acquire fast-growing, founder-led young companies.

---

critical evaluation of noncore businesses, and an improved management of costs.

A case in point is Dell, the best-performing large company of the 1990s. It began to stall out a decade later, when some of the advantages of its legendary direct sales model began to narrow, and the company saw its market value decline from $107 billion in 1999 to just under $25 billion in 2013—a 77% drop. When Michael Dell returned as CEO to renew the company he'd founded, he concluded that he could more effectively make the changes he wanted if he took the company private, which he did in partnership with Silver Lake in 2013.

"In going private," he told us, "it's amazing how we have been able to speed things up. We simplified meeting structures, went to a board of directors with just three members, and increased our appetite for risk. When big committees talk about risk, they talk about risk committees, how risk is bad, the mitigation procedures of risk, and the reaction of the analysts. For us risk is now about innovation and success. It has been very energizing to our 100,000 employees to feel the long-term focus coming back into the company."

Customer satisfaction scores have rebounded, and Dell's employee satisfaction scores are the highest in the company's history. Its core businesses are outgrowing their industry peers again, and Dell is investing heavily to redefine its model for the long term.

Going private is not for all, of course. An owner's mindset can be instilled without taking the business off the market. Companies can generate "mini-founder" experiences by, for example, creating franchises with direct ownership stakes or encouraging employees to create internal startups that might later be spun off. They can encourage investors with a more long-term focus and link executive pay more closely to long-term performance measures. They can change the timing of internal meetings to increase the speed of decision making. (Some leadership teams, for instance, hold Monday meetings and Tuesday follow-ups with the aim of removing blockages to important decisions and actions.) They can reach outside the company to partner with insurgents and perhaps eventually acquire them. Or they can bring founders into the company through acquisition and work to retain them and their entrepreneurial energy. This has been the approach of companies such as Cisco, Google, and eBay.

Initially a huge success story, and one of the first dot-coms to radically scale up, eBay stalled out in the late 2000s—a victim of Amazon and other online retail competitors and of its own diversification, which included acquiring Skype. Its aging e-commerce auction model seemed vulnerable to competitors, and its share price had fallen from $59 in 2004 to a low of $10 in 2009.

When John Donahoe became the CEO at eBay, he recognized that to get the company moving again, he would have to divest noncore businesses, revamp eBay's e-commerce platform, and, most important, shift its focus to a hotbed of innovation: mobile commerce. To successfully enter the mobile space, however, he would have to turbocharge the company's innovation pipeline and capabilities—and the only way he could manage that, he told us, would be "to fill eBay with young entrepreneurs." In doing so, he was guided by a general truth about transforming stalled-out companies: Often, outside forces need to be brought in.

Not long after he took over, Donahoe began to acquire small, founder-led companies at a rate of about one every three months. He wasn't interested solely in acquisitions and technological innovations. He wanted to retain the founders and their teams, frequently so that he could move them into core-business positions. "Many of these founders like our approach," Donahoe told us, "because they can innovate at scale in eBay, and they get to expose their innovations to 130 million customers globally."

One of them was Jack Abraham, the 25-year-old founder of Milo, a shopping engine that searched stores for the best-priced merchandise. At one of the regular Friday meetings that Donahoe held with company leaders under 30, Abraham raised his hand and proposed a major innovation for the home page. Donahoe told him to go figure out what resources he needed to explore the idea. Immediately after the meeting, Abraham found five of the best developers in the company, went out for drinks with them that night, and persuaded them to leave with him the next morning for two weeks in Australia, where they would be as isolated from California headquarters as possible and could work on developing a prototype.

What they came up with blew Donahoe away. "Had we asked a normal product team," he said, "I would have gotten back hundreds of PowerPoint slides and a two-year time frame and a budget of $40 million. Yet these guys went away, worked 24/7, and built a prototype. These guys build. They do no PowerPoint. They just build."

Obviously, Donahoe's approach is best suited to fast-moving markets where incumbents need to constantly add technologies and build new capabilities. Not all these initiatives have been lasting successes. The fivefold increase in eBay's stock price during Donahoe's tenure was driven by many things, including the success and spin-off of PayPal (whose independent status has enhanced its founder's mentality), yet it is a clear example of the power of pulling in business owners from the outside and harnessing their energy and entrepreneurialism.

———————

Stall-outs are frightening for companies—if ignored or mishandled, they can lead to lasting reversals of fortune. But like any other daunting challenge, they can also be viewed as an opportunity. When we analyzed value swings on the stock market, we found that some of the biggest upturns occur when a company is forced to return to its core and redefine it in the process. Managers need not panic when stall-out occurs. Companies that reignite their mission, renew their obsession with the front line, and instill an owner's mentality throughout the organization can reach new heights.

Originally published in March 2016. Reprint R1603F

Global Supply Chains in a Post-Pandemic World

by Willy C. Shih

WHEN THE COVID-19 PANDEMIC SUBSIDES, the world is going to look markedly different. The supply shock that started in China in February and the demand shock that followed as the global economy shut down exposed vulnerabilities in the production strategies and supply chains of firms just about everywhere. Temporary trade restrictions and shortages of pharmaceuticals, critical medical supplies, and other products highlighted their weaknesses. Those developments, combined with the U.S.-China trade war, have triggered a rise in economic nationalism. As a consequence of all this, manufacturers worldwide are going to be under greater political and competitive pressures to increase their domestic production, grow employment in their home countries, reduce or even eliminate their dependence on sources that are perceived as risky, and rethink their use of lean manufacturing strategies that involve minimizing the amount of inventory held in their global supply chains.

Yet many things are not going to change. Consumers will continue to want low prices (especially in a recession), and firms won't be able to charge more just because they manufacture in higher-cost home markets. Competition will ensure that. In addition, the pressure to operate efficiently and use capital and manufacturing capacity frugally will remain unrelenting.

The challenge for companies will be to make their supply chains more resilient without weakening their competitiveness. To meet that challenge. managers should first understand their vulnerabilities and then consider a number of steps—some of which they should have taken long before the pandemic struck.

Uncover and Address the Hidden Risks

Modern products often incorporate critical components or sophisticated materials that require specialized technological skills to make. It is very difficult for a single firm to possess the breadth of capabilities necessary to produce everything by itself. Consider the growing electronics content in modern vehicles. Automakers aren't equipped to create the touchscreen displays in the entertainment and navigation systems or the countless microprocessors that control the engine, steering, and functions such as power windows and lighting. Another more arcane example is a group of chemicals known as nucleoside phosphoramidites and the associated reagents that are used for creating DNA and RNA sequences. These are essential for all companies developing DNA- or mRNA-based Covid-19 vaccines and DNA-based drug therapies. but many of the key precursor materials come from South Korea and China.

Manufacturers in most industries have turned to suppliers and subcontractors who narrowly focus on just one area, and those specialists, in turn, usually have to rely on many others. Such an arrangement offers benefits: You have a lot of flexibility in what goes into your product, and you're able to incorporate the latest technology. But you are left vulnerable when you depend on a single supplier somewhere deep in your network for a crucial component or material. If that supplier produces the item in only one plant or one country, your disruption risks are even higher.

Identify your vulnerabilities

Understanding where the risks lie so that your company can protect itself may require a lot of digging. It entails going far beyond the first and second tiers and mapping your full supply chain,

Idea in Brief

The Problem

Disruptions and shortages during the Covid-19 pandemic exposed weaknesses in global supply chains, which already aced threats from trade wars.

The Cause

Many companies hadn't rigorously identified and addressed hidden vulnerabilities.

The Solution

Thoroughly map your supply chain to uncover risks. To mitigate them, line up alternative supply sources in diverse locations or increase stocks of critical materials. Revisit your product strategies. And explore new manufacturing technologies that could increase flexibility and resilience.

including distribution facilities and transportation hubs. This is time-consuming and expensive, which explains why most major firms have focused their attention only on strategic direct suppliers that account for large amounts of their expenditures. But a surprise disruption that brings your business to a halt can be much more costly than a deep look into your supply chain is.

The goal of the mapping process should be to categorize suppliers as low-, medium-, or high-risk. To do that, Tom Linton, who served as a supply chain executive at several major companies, and MIT's David Simchi-Levi suggest applying metrics such as the impact on revenues if a certain source is lost, the time it would take a particular supplier's factory to recover from a disruption, and the availability of alternate sources. (Disclosure: I am on the boards of directors of Flex, a large manufacturing and supply-chain services provider where Linton is a senior adviser, and Veo Robotics, a company that has developed an advanced vision and 3D sensing system for industrial robots.) It's vital to ascertain how long your company could ride out a supply shock without shutting down, and how quickly an incapacitated node could recover or be replaced by alternate sites when an entire industry faces a disruption-related shortage.

The answers to those questions depend, in part, on whether your manufacturing capacity is flexible and can be reconfigured and redeployed as needs evolve (as is the case for many manual or semiautomated assembly operations) or whether it consists of highly specialized and difficult-to-replicate operations. Examples of the latter include production of the most advanced smartphone chips, which is concentrated in three facilities in Taiwan owned by the Taiwan Semiconductor Manufacturing Company; fabrication of exotic sensors and components, which happens largely in highly specialized facilities in a handful of countries, including Japan, Germany, and the United States; and refining of neodymium for the magnets in AirPods and electric-vehicle motors, almost all of which is done in China.

Once you've identified the risks in your supply chain, you can use that information to address them by either diversifying your sources or stockpiling key materials or items.

Diversify your supply base

The obvious way to address heavy dependence on one medium- or high-risk source (a single factory, supplier, or region) is to add more sources in locations not vulnerable to the same risks. The U.S.-China trade war has motivated some firms to shift to a "China plus one" strategy of spreading production between China and a Southeast Asian country such as Vietnam, Indonesia, or Thailand. But region-wide problems like the 1997 Asian financial crisis or the 2004 tsunami argue for broader geographic diversification.

Managers should consider a regional strategy of producing a substantial proportion of key goods within the region where they are consumed. North America might be served by shifting labor-intensive work from China to Mexico and Central America. To supply Western Europe with items used there, companies could increase their reliance on eastern EU countries, Turkey, and Ukraine. Chinese firms that want to protect their global market share are already looking to Egypt, Ethiopia, Kenya, Myanmar, and Sri Lanka for low-tech, labor-intensive production.

Reducing dependency on China will be easier for some products than others. Things like furniture, clothing, and household goods will be relatively easy to obtain elsewhere because the inputs— lumber, fabrics, plastics, and so forth—are basic materials. It will be harder to find alternative source for sophisticated machinery, electronics, and other goods that incorporate components such as high-density interconnect circuit boards, electronic displays, and precision castings.

Building a new supplier infrastructure in a different country or region will take considerable time and money, as China's experience illustrates. When China first opened its special economic zones in the 1980s, it had almost no indigenous suppliers and had to rely on far-flung global supply chains and on logistics specialists who procured materials from around the world and kitted them for assembly in Chinese factories. Even with the support of government incentives, it took 20 years for the country to build a local base capable of supplying the vast majority of electronic components, auto parts, chemicals, and drug ingredients needed for domestic manufacturing.

Shifting production from China to Southeast Asian countries will necessitate different logistics strategies as well. Unlike China, those locations often do not have the efficient, high-capacity ports that can handle the largest container ships or the direct marine liner services to major markets. That will mean more transshipment through Singapore, Hong Kong, or other hubs and longer transit times to reach markets.

In the long run, though, it would be a mistake to cut China completely out of your supply picture. The country's deep supplier networks, its flexible and able workforce, and its large and efficient ports and transportation infrastructure mean that it will remain a highly competitive source for years to come. And because China has the second-largest economy in the world, it is important that firms maintain a presence to sell in its markets and obtain competitive intelligence.

Hold intermediate inventory or safety stock

If alternate suppliers are not immediately available, a company should determine how much extra stock to hold in the interim, in what form, and where along the value chain. Of course, safety stock, like any inventory, carries with it the risk of obsolescence and also ties up cash. It runs counter to the popular practice of just-in-time replenishment and lean inventories. But the savings from those practices have to be weighed against all the costs of a disruption, including lost revenues, the higher prices that would have to be paid for materials that are suddenly in short supply, and the time and effort that would be required to secure them.

Take Advantage of Process Innovations

As firms relocate parts of their supply chain, some might ask their suppliers to move with them, or they might bring some production back in-house. Either course—transplanting a production line or setting up a new one—is an opportunity to make major process improvements. This is because as part of the change, you can unfreeze your organizational routines and revisit design assumptions underpinning the original process. (One challenge for companies with existing production lines is that when those assets are fully depreciated, executives may be tempted to retain them rather than invest in newer, more competitive plants and equipment: Since the depreciation expense is no longer factored into the calculated cost of production, the marginal cost of boosting production at a plant with idle capacity is lower.)

Several years ago I spent a week at a new Chinese factory of a major American industrial-equipment company. When creating it, the company had started with the designs of its U.S. and Japanese factories and then improved on them by introducing newer equipment and ways of working. The result was a streamlined operation that was much more efficient than those in the United States and Japan. When the company built its next new factory—in the United States—it repeated the process, using the Chinese factory as the starting point. Another example is the Flex factory complex in Guadalajara, Mexico. When increases in productivity plateaued, the company often moved smaller assembly lines to another building (or part of the same building). During each move, workers redesigned steps to use less space and less labor, boosting productivity.

Further Reading

"Bringing Manufacturing Back to the U.S. Is Easier Said Than Done," Willy C. Shih, hbr.org, April 15, 2020

"It's Up to Manufacturers to Keep Their Suppliers Afloat," Tom Linton and Bindiya Vakil, hbr.org, April 14, 2020

"Coronavirus Is a Wake-Up Call for Supply Chain Management," Thomas Y. Choi, Dale Rogers, and Bindiya Vakil, hbr.org, March 27, 2020

"Coronavirus Is Proving We Need More Resilient Supply Chains," Tom Linton and Bindiya Vakil, hbr.org, March 5, 2020

"The 3-D Printing Playbook," Richard A. D'Aveni, HBR, July–August 2018

"Find the Weak Link in Your Supply Chain," David Simchi-Levi, hbr.org, June 9, 2015

"From Superstorms to Factory Fires: Managing Unpredictable Supply-Chain Disruptions," David Simchi-Levi, William Schmidt, and Yehua Wei, HBR, January–February 2014

"Innovation Killers: How Financial Tools Destroy Your Capacity to Do New Things," Clayton M. Christensen, Stephen P. Kaufman, and Willy C. Shih, HBR, January 2008

"Does America Really Need Manufacturing?" Gary P. Pisano and Willy C. Shih, HBR, March 2012

"Restoring American Competitiveness," Gary P. Pisano and Willy C. Shih, HBR, July–August 2009

New technologies already or soon will allow companies to lower their costs or switch more flexibly among the products they manufacture, rendering obsolete the installed bases of incumbent competitors or suppliers. Many of these advances also present an opportunity to make factories more environmentally sustainable. Examples include the following:

Automation: As the cost of automation declines and people see that robots can operate safely alongside humans, more kinds of work are being automated. The pandemic has made automation even more attractive, because social distancing in factories is now a necessity. As a result of these developments, it's becoming more practical to return off-shored production to higher-cost countries. Robotic palletizers, which can sharply reduce the need for labor in preparing products for shipping, will pay for themselves quickly, as will automated optical inspection systems for quality control.

New processing technologies: The latest chemical manufacturing equipment uses less energy and solvents, produces less waste, is less capital-intensive, and is less expensive to operate. Similarly, a new generation of compact bioreactors could allow makers of biopharmaceuticals and vaccines to produce smaller batch sizes economically.

Continuous-flow manufacturing: This innovation could significantly increase the resilience of the supply chain for small-molecule generic drugs by making producers less dependent on imported active pharmaceutical ingredients (APIs). The U.S. Defense Advanced Research Projects Agency (DARPA) has funded one initiative in this area: the development of flexible miniaturized manufacturing platforms and methods for producing multiple APIs from shelf-stable precursors as specific medical needs arise.

Additive manufacturing: This production method, also known as 3D printing, can dramatically reduce the number of steps required to make complex metal shapes; it can also lessen dependence on distant suppliers of the machinery and tools needed for, say, the injection molding of plastics. Rapid advances in 3D printing are making it possible to economically produce an ever-expanding array of items in much higher quantities.

In many industries, technologies such as these promise to upend the traditional strategy of seeking economies of scale by concentrating production in a few large facilities. They will allow companies to replace large plants that serve global markets with a network of smaller, geographically distributed factories that is more resistant to disruption.

Revisit the Trade-Off Between Product Variety and Capacity Flexibility

During the pandemic, when demand surged in many product categories, manufacturers struggled to shift from supplying one market segment to supplying another, or from making one kind of product to making another. A case in point is the U.S. groceries market, where companies had difficulty adjusting to the plunge in demand from restaurants and cafeterias and the rise in consumer demand. SKU proliferation—the addition of different forms of the same product to serve different market segments—was partly responsible. For example, one obstacle to meeting heightened demand for toilet paper at supermarkets was that manufacturers had to change over their production lines, because consumers prefer soft multi-ply rolls rather than the thinner toilet paper that many hotels and offices purchased in much larger rolls. Adding to the complexity, different retail chains wanted their own packaging and assortments.

Researchers such as Barry Schwartz of Swarthmore College and Patrick Spenner, a consultant who was formerly at CEB (now part of Gartner), have long argued that more choice isn't always better. Separating demand into many different SKUs makes forecasting more difficult, and trying to fill needs by substituting products during periods of shortage causes a real scramble. The lesson: Companies should reconsider the pros and cons of producing numerous product variations.

The economic turmoil caused by the pandemic has exposed many vulnerabilities in supply chains and raised doubts about globalization. Managers everywhere should use this crisis to take a fresh look at their supply networks, take steps to understand their vulnerabilities, and then take actions to improve robustness. They can't and shouldn't totally back away from globalization; doing so will leave avoid that others—companies that *don't* abandon globalization—will gladly and quickly fill. Instead, leaders should find ways to make their businesses work better and give themselves an advantage. It's time to adopt a new vision suitable to the realities of the new era—one that still leverages the capabilities that reside around the world but also improves resilience and reduces the risks from future disruptions that are certain to occur.

Originally published in September–October 2020. Reprint R2005F

Roaring Out of Recession

by Ranjay Gulati, Nitin Nohria, and Franz Wohlgezogen

GREAT LEADERS KNOW that how they fight a war often decides whether they will win the peace. Yet as CEOs continue to combat the myriad challenges thrown up by the Great Recession of 2007, they are increasingly unsure about what strategic approaches to deploy. Many worry that the 27-month slowdown is far from over in the United States. Others feel that although a recovery may have begun, it could prove to be short-lived, and they would do well to brace for a double-dip recession. Almost all business leaders reluctantly admit that the current crisis also marks an inflection point: The world after it is unlikely to resemble the one before it. Their priority, when they get a moment's respite, must be to remake their organizations to cope with the "new normal." But CEOs, like generals in the heat of battle, are so busy tackling short-term priorities that the future is obscured by the fog of war.

Unfortunately, little research has been done on strategies that can help companies survive a recession, get ahead during a slow-growth recovery, and be ready to win when good times return. Folksy wisdom abounds (how many times have you read that Procter & Gamble, Chevy, and Camel flourished during the Great Depression because they advertised heavily?), but empirical studies are few. That's why we decided to mount a yearlong project to analyze strategy selection and corporate performance during the past three global recessions: the 1980 crisis (which lasted from 1980 to 1982), the 1990 slowdown (1990 to 1991), and the 2000 bust (2000 to 2002). We studied 4,700 public companies, breaking down the data into three periods: the three years before a recession, the three years after, and the recession years themselves. (See the sidebar "Analyzing Strategy Shifts.")

Our findings are stark and startling. Seventeen percent of the companies in our study didn't survive a recession: They went bankrupt, were acquired, or became private. The survivors were painfully slow to recover from the battering. About 80% of them had not yet regained their prerecession growth rates for sales and profits three years after a recession; in fact, 40% of them hadn't even returned to their absolute prerecession sales and profits levels by the end of that time period. Only a small number of companies—approximately 9% of our sample—flourished after a slowdown, doing better on key financial parameters than they had before it and outperforming rivals in their industry by at least 10% in terms of sales and profits growth.

These postrecession winners aren't the usual suspects. Firms that cut costs faster and deeper than rivals don't necessarily flourish. They have the lowest probability—21%—of pulling ahead of the competition when times get better, according to our study. Businesses that boldly invest more than their rivals during a recession don't always fare well either. They enjoy only a 26% chance of becoming leaders after a downturn. And companies that were growth leaders coming into a recession often can't retain their momentum; about 85% are toppled during bad times.

Just who *are* the postrecession winners? What strategies do they deploy? Can other corporations emulate them? According to our research, companies that master the delicate balance between cutting costs to survive today and investing to grow tomorrow do well after a recession. Within this group, a subset that deploys a specific combination of defensive and offensive moves has the highest probability—37%—of breaking away from the pack. These companies reduce costs selectively by focusing more on operational efficiency than their rivals do, even as they invest relatively comprehensively in the future by spending on marketing, R&D, and new assets. Their

Idea in Brief

What strategies can companies use to survive a recession so that they'll thrive when it ends? A yearlong study suggests that enterprises that cut costs by focusing on operating efficiency even as they spend more than rivals on marketing, R&D, and assets are likely to be postrecession winners.

Companies that only cut costs heavily during a downturn don't flourish after it ends. Neither do the few businesses that only invest more than rivals during a recession.

Even companies that were doing well beforehand don't retain their momentum—85% of market leaders get dislodged during a recession.

Cutting costs while making investments isn't easy. CEOs must be disciplined about costs and learn to spot investment opportunities that offer reliable returns in reasonable payback periods. If they get the mix right, it helps them tackle short-run problems and create a successful medium-term strategy.

multipronged strategy, which we will discuss in the following pages, is the best antidote to a recession.

Four Responses to a Slowdown

Companies, not surprisingly, don't all follow the same strategies during a recession. That could be because of differences in executives' cognitive orientation during a crisis. According to Tory Higgins, a Columbia University psychologist, human beings are hedonistic— we avoid pain and seek pleasure—but they differ in how they try to achieve those aims. There are two basic modes of self-regulation. Some people are driven most by goals, such as achievement, advancement, and growth. These promotion-focused individuals are motivated by ideals and aspirations that provide pleasure if realized and disappointment if not. Other people are prevention-focused—concerned mainly with safety, security, and responsibility. They strive to avoid bad outcomes, experiencing relief if they succeed and pain if they fail. Situations have a potent influence on cognitive orientation: A recession, for example, can trigger a response that overrides a person's usual orientation.

By applying this perspective to our empirical research, we were able to classify companies and their approaches to managing during a recession into four types:

Prevention-focused companies, which make primarily defensive moves and are more concerned than their rivals with avoiding losses and minimizing downside risks.

Promotion-focused companies, which invest more in offensive moves that provide upside benefits than their peers do.

Pragmatic companies, which combine defensive and offensive moves.

Progressive companies, which deploy the optimal combination of defense and offense.

Let's now analyze these groups.

Don't Be Too Defensive

Confronted by a recession, many CEOs swing into crisis mode, believing that their sole responsibility is to prevent the company from getting badly hurt or going under. They quickly implement policies that will reduce operating costs, shrink discretionary expenditures, eliminate frills, rationalize business portfolios, lower head count, and preserve cash. They also postpone making fresh investments in R&D, developing new businesses, or buying assets such as plants and machinery. As a rule, prevention-focused leaders cut back on almost every item of cost and investment and reduce expenditures significantly more than their competitors on at least one dimension.

Sony, which announced a cost-reduction target of $2.6 billion in December 2008, epitomizes the prevention-focused approach. It plans to close several factories and eliminate 16,000 jobs, and will delay investments—such as building a much-needed LCD television factory in Slovakia—in its core electronics business. This strategy resembles the approach Sony took during the 2000 downturn, when over a two-year period the Japanese giant cut its workforce by 11%, its R&D expenditures by 12%, and its capital expenditures by 23%. The cuts helped Sony increase its profit margin from 8% in 1999 to 12% in 2002, but growth in its sales tumbled from an average of 11%

in the three years before the recession to 1% thereafter. In fact, Sony has struggled since then to regain momentum. It has invested in developing new products such as electronic book readers, gaming consoles, and organic light-emitting diode TV sets, but finds itself bested in those product categories by Amazon, Microsoft and Nintendo, and Samsung, respectively.

A focus solely on cost cutting causes several problems. One, executives and employees start approaching every decision through a loss-minimizing lens. A siege mentality leads the organization to aim low and keep both innovation and cost cutting incremental. Two, instead of learning to operate more efficiently, the organization tries to do more of the same with less. That often results in lower quality and therefore a drop in customer satisfaction. Three, cost-cutting decisions become centralized: The finance department makes across-the-board cuts, paying little attention to initiatives that may be the nuclei of postrecession growth. Four, pessimism permeates the organization. Centralization, strict controls, and the constant threat of more cuts build a feeling of disempowerment. The focus becomes survival—both personal and organizational.

Few prevention-focused corporations do well after a recession, according to our study. They trail the other groups, with growth, on average, of 6% in sales and 4% in profits, compared with 13% and 12% for progressive companies. Whereas in the three years after the 2000 recession, sales for the 200 largest companies grew by an average of $12 billion over prerecession levels, the prevention-focused enterprises among them saw sales grow by an average of just $5 billion. Moreover, cost cutting didn't lead to above-average growth in earnings. Postrecession profits for prevention-focused enterprises typically rose by only $600 million, whereas for progressive companies they increased by an average of $6.6 billion.

Don't Be Too Aggressive

Some business leaders pursue opportunity even in the face of adversity. They use a recession as a pretext to push change through, get closer to customers who may be ignored by competitors, make

Analyzing Strategy Shifts

IN DECEMBER 2008 we started a project to identify the strategies that companies deploy during economic downturns and to evaluate their effectiveness. We studied corporate performance during the three recessionary periods prior to the current one: 1980 to 1982, 1990 to 1991, and 2000 to 2002.

We collected financial data on all the companies listed in Standard & Poor's Compustat database, analyzing 4,700 companies across the three recessions. Using data for the three years prior to each recession, the three years after it, and the recession itself, we analyzed strategy shifts during the recession years and developed hypotheses about how they had affected companies' postrecession performance.

To identify strategy shifts, we calculated how companies' resource allocations had changed between the prerecession and the recession years, using six balance-sheet items: number of employees; cost of goods sold normalized by sales; R&D expenditures; sales, general, and administrative expenditures; capital expenditures; and plant, property, and equipment stock.

Only major allocation changes affect a company's performance, so we isolated those in two steps: first, we calculated changes from before to during each recession and adjusted them for the industry average; second, we calculated the percentile scores of those changes and assumed that only those in the top or bottom 33 percentile were significant increases or decreases.

We identified four groups on the basis of specific combinations of changes in resource allocation:

Prevention-focused companies, which had cut back further, relative to their competitors, on one or more of the six items, and hadn't increased expenditures on any of them more than their competitors had.

---

strategic investments that have long-term payoffs, and act opportunistically to acquire talent, assets, or businesses that become available during the downturn. These strategies are designed to garner upside benefits.

At the height of the 2000 recession, for example, Hewlett-Packard drew up an ambitious change agenda even though sales and profits were falling. Carly Fiorina, then the CEO, asserted, "In blackjack, you double down when you have an increasing probability of winning. We're going to double down." HP embarked on a massive restructuring program, made the largest acquisition in its history by

Promotion-focused companies, which had increased expenditure on at least one of the six and also not decreased expenditure on any of them by more than their rivals had.

Pragmatic companies, which had adopted both a prevention focus, by reducing COGS or employees more than their peers had, and a promotion focus, by increasing SG&A, R&D, CAPX, or PP&E more than their peers had.

Progressive companies, which had reduced COGS but hadn't cut employees more than their peers and had also allocated more resources, relative to their competitors, to market-related items such as SG&A and R&D and to asset-related items such as CAPX and PP&E.

We then calculated the three-year compound annual growth rates for net sales and earnings (EBITDA as a percentage of sales), adjusted for industry averages, to understand the top- and bottom-line performance generated by these strategies. Using growth rates allowed us to compare the performance of big and small companies; by adjusting for industry averages, we could compare performance across industries even if the recession had affected them differently.

We concluded that companies with both sales growth and profits growth 10% higher than those of competitors after a recession had achieved breakaway performance. (Our findings are valid, however, for a broad range of definitions of breakaway performance: growth rates from 5% to 20% better than the industry average.)

Finally, we calculated the probability that companies in each of the four groups would achieve breakaway performance by dividing the number of winning companies that had used a certain strategy by the total number of companies using that strategy.

buying Compaq for $25 billion, and increased R&D expenditures by 9%. It also spent $200 million on a corporate branding campaign and $1 billion on expanding the availability of information technology in developing countries. These initiatives strained the organization and spread top management's attention too thin. When the recession ended, the company found it tough to match the profitability levels of IBM and Dell. By 2004 HP's earnings, at 8.4%, had slipped below IBM's 16.8% and Dell's 9.3%. (Throughout this article, "profits" and "earnings" refer to earnings before interest, taxes, depreciation, and amortization [EBITDA] as a percentage of sales.)

What are the odds . . .

that companies in the four groups will significantly outperform their rivals (by 10% or more) on both top- and bottom-line growth after a recession?

21%
Prevention focus

26%
Promotion focus

29%
Pragmatic focus

37%
Progressive focus

Organizations that focus purely on promotion develop a culture of optimism that leads them to deny the gravity of a crisis for a long time. They ignore early warning signs, such as customers' budget cuts, and are steadfast in the belief that as long as they innovate, their sales and profits will continue to rise. Even as customers clamor for lower prices and greater value for money, these companies add bells and whistles to their products. They simply don't notice that because the pie is shrinking, they must capture an even larger share from rivals to keep growing. Optimistic leaders attract employees who thrive in a forward-looking, growth-oriented environment. When positive groupthink permeates an organization, naysayers are marginalized and realities are overlooked. That's why promotion-focused organizations are often blindsided by poor financial results.

Worse, when these companies are forced to tackle bloated cost structures, the changes they make often prove to be too little, too late. Because each function and business firmly believes that it contributes to corporate success, finger-pointing increases. Trade-offs are difficult to make and decision making becomes sclerotic.

Whereas prevention-oriented companies lower their cost-to-sales ratio by about three percentage points relative to peers over the course of a recession, promotion-focused enterprises are unable to reduce that ratio. Promotion-focused CEOs sometimes increase expenditures rather than cutting back, believing that this will push them ahead. If investments take longer than expected to generate paybacks, or innovations don't resonate with customers, these companies run headlong into trouble.

Despite a focus on growth, promotion-focused companies' postrecession sales and earnings rise by only 8% and 6% respectively, whereas those of progressive companies' shoot up by 13% and 12%. Among the 200 largest companies that tackled the 2000 recession, promotion-focused enterprises grew sales by $15 billion and profits by $1.5 billion, on average—far lower than progressive companies' average increases of $28 billion in sales and $6.6 billion in profits.

The Elusive Balance

The companies most likely to outperform their competitors after a recession are pragmatic as William James defined the term: "The attitude of looking away from first things, principles, 'categories,' supposed necessities; and of looking towards last things, fruits, consequences, facts." The CEOs of pragmatic companies recognize that cost cutting is necessary to survive a recession, that investment is equally essential to spur growth, and that they must manage both at the same time if their companies are to emerge as postrecession leaders.

A combination strategy sounds easy to develop: a little offense, a little defense, and voilà, you're a winner. If only it were that simple. Companies typically combine three defensive approaches—reducing the number of employees, improving operational efficiency, or both—with three offensive ones: developing new markets, investing in new assets, or both. This yields nine possible combinations, some of which are more effective than others. (See the exhibit "What's the best combination of moves?")

One combination has the greatest likelihood of producing postrecession winners: the one pursued by progressive enterprises. These companies' defensive moves are selective. They cut costs mainly by improving operational efficiency rather than by slashing the number of employees relative to peers. However, their offensive moves are comprehensive. They develop new business opportunities by making significantly greater investments than their rivals do in R&D and marketing, and they invest in assets such as plants and machinery. Their postrecession growth in sales and earnings is the best among the groups in our study. It's important to understand why the companies that use this combination do so well after a recession.

Operational efficiency

Most enterprises implement aggressive cost-reduction plans to survive a recession. But companies that attend to improving operational efficiency fare better than those that focus on reducing the number of employees. Don't get us wrong: Progressive companies also lay off employees, but they rely on that approach much less than their peers do. Only 23% of progressive enterprises cut staff—whereas 56% of prevention-focused companies do—and they lay off far fewer people.

Companies that rely solely on cutting the workforce have only an 11% probability of achieving breakaway performance after a downturn. There may be several reasons for this. In our experience, morale is usually better at companies that stress operational efficiency. Employees at these companies appreciate top management's commitment to them, and they are more creative in reducing costs as a result. They don't spend their time worrying about job security—as do people at companies that rely on deep staff cuts. And although layoffs may reduce costs quickly, they make recovery more difficult. Companies run the risk of scaling up too late, especially if hiring is more difficult than they anticipated. People are loath to work for organizations that reduce head count in difficult times. Moreover, as these companies rehire, costs shoot up.

In contrast, companies that respond to a slowdown by reexamining every aspect of their business models—from how they have configured supply chains to how they are organized and structured—reduce their operating costs on a permanent basis. When demand returns, costs will stay low, allowing their profits to grow faster than those of competitors.

What's the best combination of moves?

Companies that focus simultaneously on increasing operational efficiency, developing new markets, and enlarging their asset bases show the strongest performance, on average, in sales and EBITDA growth after a recession. (Percentages, which are adjusted for industry averages, refer to the three-year compound annual growth rate.)

		Promotion-focused moves		
		Market development	Asset investment	Both
Prevention-focused moves	Employee reduction	**Good** Sales 4.6% EBITDA 6.6%	**Bad** Sales 3.9% EBITDA 3.3%	**Worst** Sales 3.3% EBITDA -5.2%
	Operational efficiency	**Good** Sales 7.1% EBITDA 4.2%	**Good** Sales 8.4% EBITDA 8.4%	**Best** Sales 13.0% EBITDA 12.2%
	Both	**Bad** Sales 5.2% EBITDA 2.1%	**Bad** Sales 5.2% EBITDA -0.5%	**Good** Sales 9.2% EBITDA 4.6%

During the 2000 recession, Office Depot and Staples took differing approaches to cost management. Office Depot cut 6% of its workforce, but it couldn't reduce operating costs significantly. Although the company created an incentive plan to boost sales, its sales growth fell from 19% before the recession to 8% after—five percentage points below Staples' postrecession sales growth rate.

By contrast, Staples closed down some underperforming facilities but increased its workforce by 10% during the recession, mainly to support the high-end product categories and services it introduced. At the same time, the company contained its operating costs and came out of the recession stronger, bigger, and more profitable than it had been in 1999. Its sales doubled, from $7.1 billion in 1997 to $14.6 billion in 2003, while Office Depot's rose by about 50%, from

$8.7 billion to $13.4 billion. On average, Staples was about 30% more profitable than its archrival in the three years after that recession.

Investment in both existing and new businesses

During recessions, progressive companies develop new markets and invest to enlarge their asset bases. They take advantage of depressed prices to buy property, plants, and equipment. This helps them both during the recession and afterward, when they can respond faster than rivals to a rise in demand. Because their asset costs are lower than their noninvesting competitors', their earnings can be relatively higher.

These companies also judiciously increase spending on R&D and marketing, which may produce only modest benefits during the recession, but adds substantially to sales and profits afterward. The resources freed up by improving operational efficiency finance much of this expenditure. In turbulent times, it's tough for companies to know where to place their bets for both the immediate term and the long run. Progressive companies stay closely connected to customer needs—a powerful filter through which to make investment decisions.

Getting It Right

Pursuing a Janus-faced strategy isn't easy. Cutting budgets in one area while expanding them in another means explaining to those who are being asked to bear the burden of the former why the company is spending where no immediate benefits are apparent. It's easier to exhort everyone to sacrifice and share the pain or to show courage and invest for gain. To pull off a combination of cutbacks and strategic investments, CEOs have to exercise cost discipline and financial prudence and detect opportunities that offer reliable returns in reasonable payback periods.

Let's look at how one company has managed this difficult balancing act. During the 2000 recession, Target increased its marketing and sales expenditures by 20% and its capital expenditures

Postrecession leaders in sales and profits growth

After a recession, progressive companies outperform pragmatic companies by almost four percentage points in sales and more than three percentage points in earnings before interest, taxes, depreciation, and amortization (EBITDA)—and do about twice as well as companies in general. (Percentages, which are adjusted for industry averages, refer to the three-year compound annual growth rate.)

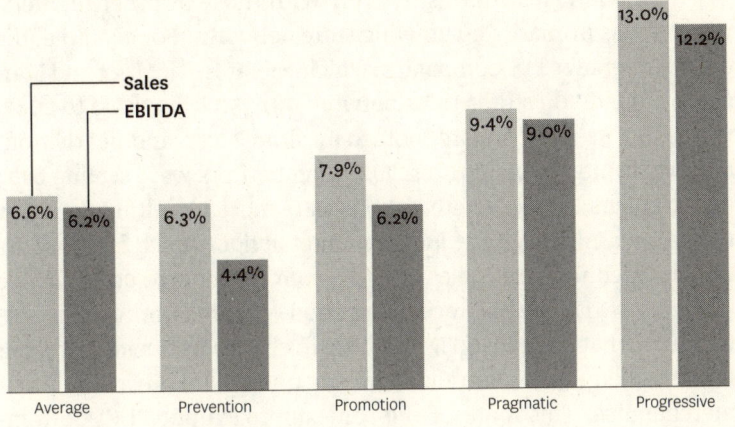

by 50% over prerecession levels. It increased the number of stores it operated from 947 to 1,107 and added 88 Super-Target stores to the 30 it had already set up. It expanded into several new merchandise segments, ramped up investment in credit-card programs, and grew its internet business. The company made several smart choices along the way. Instead of trying to go it alone online, Target partnered with Amazon to sell its products. It also teamed up with well-known designers such as Michael Graves, Philippe Starck, and Todd Oldham to cement its reputation for cheap chic, thereby differentiating its products.

Meanwhile, Target relentlessly tried to reduce costs, improve productivity, and enhance the efficiency of its supply chain operations.

For instance, in 2000 it was one of the 12 retailers that founded the WorldWide Retail Exchange, a global business-to-business electronic marketplace, to facilitate trading between retailers and vendors. In January 2001 Target consolidated its Dayton's and Hudson's stores under Marshall Field's to take advantage of the well-known brand name. These moves helped the company grow sales by 40% and profits by 50% over the course of the recession. Its profit margin increased from 9% in the three years before the recession to 10% after it.

These strategies contrast sharply with those of other retailers, which focus primarily on growing store networks. For example, the discount retailer TJX Companies, which operates T.J. Maxx and Marshalls, added 300 stores to its network of 1,350 from 2000 to 2002, increasing its retail square footage by almost 25% and nearly doubling its capital expenditures. TJX's competitors were scaling back growth plans, so real estate options were more plentiful and prices were lower. Although the increase in retail floor space fueled some healthy medium-term sales growth—four percentage points above peers' growth in the postrecession period—it didn't improve the bottom line. That's because TJX did little to change its business model; it just scaled up its centralized buying and flexible distribution of merchandise. This more-of-the-same approach put TJX's bottom-line growth, which had been on a par with rivals' before the recession, at 9% lower three years afterward.

Many CEOs find investing in bargain-basement assets a tempting offensive move in a downturn. But the revenues and profits from opportunistic investments can take a long time to materialize, leaving a company saddled with an asset base that doesn't significantly boost returns. As TJX found, focusing purely on assets also keeps companies from looking for more-imaginative ways to build new businesses that will drive growth when the recession is over.

Target hasn't faced this problem. During the current recession, the retailer initially saw a decline in same-store sales, in part because WalMart's message of everyday low prices went down well with customers. Realizing that spending on "wants" was decreasing sharply, Target strengthened its position in a key "needs" segment: food. It launched a new store format that doubles the amount of floor space devoted to food; extended the range of its food brands, Market Pantry and Archer Farms; and overhauled its operations to support the emphasis on food. The retailer also increased media spending and reaffirmed its positioning with the slogan "Expect more, pay less"—with an emphasis on the second half. These are early days, but the results appear promising: By 2008 Market Pantry's sales had increased by 30% and Archer Farms' by 13%. And food has become a $1.8 billion business for Target.

Few progressive business leaders have a master plan when they enter a recession. They encourage their organizations to discover what works and combine those findings in a portfolio of initiatives that improve efficiency along with market and asset development. This agility, even as leaders hold the course toward long-term growth and profitability, serves organizations well during a recession. An analysis of the stock market performance of companies that use progressive strategies reveals that they can also ride the momentum after a recession is over. Their approach doesn't just combat a downturn; it can lay the foundation for continued success once the downturn ends.

Originally published in March 2010. Reprint R1003C

About the Contributors

JAMES ALLEN is a partner in Bain & Company's London office and a cohead of the firm's global strategy practice. He also leads Bain's Founder's Mentality 100 initiative. He is a coauthor of a number of bestselling books, including *Profit from the Core* and *The Founder's Mentality: How to Overcome the Predictable Crises of Growth* (Harvard Business Review Press, June 2016).

JOSEPH L. BOWER is the Donald Kirk David Professor Emeritus at Harvard Business School and coauthor of the HBR article "Global Capitalism at Risk: What Are You Doing About It?" and the book *Capitalism at Risk: Rethinking the Role of Business* (Harvard Business Review Press, 2011).

CLAYTON M. CHRISTENSEN was the Kim B. Clark Professor of Business Administration at Harvard Business School and a frequent contributor to *Harvard Business Review*.

DIANE COUTU is the director of client communications at Banyan Family Business Advisors, headquartered in Cambridge, Massachusetts.

ANGELA L. DUCKWORTH is the Christopher H. Browne Distinguished Professor of Psychology at the University of Pennsylvania and the founder and CEO of Character Lab. She is the author of *Grit: The Power of Passion and Perseverance* (Scribner, 2016).

JANE E. DUTTON is the Robert L. Kahn Distinguished University Professor of Business Administration and Psychology at the University of Michigan's Ross School of Business. She is cofounder of the Center for Positive Organizations at Ross.

PETER J. FROST was cofounder of the Compassion Lab and a professor of organizational behavior at the University of British Columbia's Sauder School of Business for almost three decades.

GRETCHEN GAVETT is a senior editor at *Harvard Business Review*.

DELPHINE GIBASSIER is an associate professor of accounting for sustainable development at Audencia Business School, with 18 years of experience in financial and nonfinancial accounting. She holds a PhD from HEC Paris.

RANJAY GULATI is the Jaime and Josefina Chua Tiampo Professor of Business Administration, the head of the organizational behavior unit, and the chair of the Advanced Management Program at Harvard Business School.

JIM HACKETT is the CEO of Ford Motor Company.

GARY HAMEL is a visiting professor at London Business School and the founder of the Management Lab. He is a coauthor of *Humanocracy: Creating Organizations as Amazing as the People Inside Them* (Harvard Business Review Press, 2020).

JASON M. KANOV is an associate professor in the College of Business and Economics at Western Washington University.

THOMAS H. LEE, is the chief medical officer of Press Ganey. He is a practicing internist and a professor (part-time) of medicine at Harvard Medical School and a professor of health policy and management at the Harvard T. H. Chan School of Public Health.

JACOBA M. LILIUS is an associate professor in the Employment Relations Program at Queen's University.

ROGER L. MARTIN is the director of the Martin Prosperity Institute and a former dean of the Rotman School of Management at the University of Toronto. He is a coauthor of *Creating Great Choices: A Leader's Guide to Integrative Thinking* (Harvard Business Review Press, 2017).

DANIEL MCGINN is an executive editor at HBR, and the author of *Psyched Up: How the Science of Mental Preparation Can Help You Succeed* (Portfolio, 2017).

NITIN NOHRIA is dean of Harvard Business School.

LAURA PALMEIRO is the senior adviser to the United Nations Global Compact. She has extensive experience in finance, controlling, and sustainability at PwC and Danone. She holds an MBA from IAE Argentina.

J. PETER SCOBLIC is a cofounder and principal of Event Horizon Strategies, a foresight consultancy, and a senior fellow in the International Security Program at New America. He completed a doctorate at Harvard Business School, where his work on strategy and uncertainty won the Wyss Award for Excellence in Doctoral Research.

WILLY C. SHIH is the Robert and Jane Cizik Professor of Management Practice in Business Administration at Harvard Business School.

LIISA VÄLIKANGAS is a research affiliate at the Institute for the Future (IFTF). In addition, she teaches innovation management at Aalto University in Helsinki, Finland. She is a cofounder of Innovation Democracy, Inc., a nonprofit that supports innovative entrepreneurship in extreme environments.

ANDREW WINSTON is the coauthor of the bestseller *Green to Gold* and the author of *Green Recovery* and *The Big Pivot*. He advises some of the world's leading companies on how they can navigate and profit from environmental and social challenges.

FRANZ WOHLGEZOGEN is a senior lecturer of leadership and management at the University of Melbourne and a senior research fellow at the Centre for Workplace Leadership.

MONICA C. WORLINE is coauthor of *Awakening Compassion at Work*, a research scientist at Stanford University's Center for Compassion and Altruism Research and Education, and the CEO of EnlivenWork.

CHRIS ZOOK is a partner in Bain & Company's Boston office and has been a cohead of the firm's global strategy practice for twenty years. He is a coauthor of a number of bestselling books, including *Profit from the Core* and *The Founder's Mentality: How to Overcome the Predictable Crises of Growth* (Harvard Business Review Press, June 2016).

Index

Engage with HBR content the way you want, on any device.

With HBR's new subscription plans, you can access world-renowned **case studies** from Harvard Business School and receive **four free eBooks**. Download and customize prebuilt **slide decks and graphics** from our **Visual Library**. With HBR's archive, top 50 best-selling articles, and five new articles every day, HBR is more than just a magazine.

Subscribe Today
hbr.org/success

The most important management ideas all in one place.

We hope you enjoyed this book from *Harvard Business Review*. Now you can get even more with HBR's 10 Must Reads Boxed Set. From books on leadership and strategy to managing yourself and others, this 6-book collection delivers articles on the most essential business topics to help you succeed.

HBR's 10 Must Reads Series

The definitive collection of ideas and best practices on our most sought-after topics from the best minds in business.

- Change Management
- Collaboration
- Communication
- Emotional Intelligence
- Innovation
- Leadership
- Making Smart Decisions

- Managing Across Cultures
- Managing People
- Managing Yourself
- Strategic Marketing
- Strategy
- Teams
- The Essentials

hbr.org/mustreads